Behavioral Insights for Policy Design

Guilherme Lichand • Amiris de Paula Serdeira
Bruno Rizardi

Behavioral Insights for Policy Design

A New Framework for Understanding Wicked Social Problems and Designing Policies for Real Citizens

Springer

Guilherme Lichand
Stanford Graduate School of Education
Stanford University
Palo Alto, CA, USA

Bruno Rizardi
Catálise Social
Brasília, Brazil

Amiris de Paula Serdeira
Natura Institute
São Paulo, São Paulo, Brazil

ISBN 978-3-031-33033-9 ISBN 978-3-031-33034-6 (eBook)
https://doi.org/10.1007/978-3-031-33034-6

This Springer imprint is published by the registered company Springer Nature Switzerland AG
The registered company address is: Gewerbestrasse 11, 6330 Cham, Switzerland

Preface

The inspiration for this book stems from a common interest among the authors in expanding the public management toolkit to handle "wicked" social problems – those not very responsive to traditional public policy instruments. Think about reliance on single-use plastics, low take-up of preventive health care (even when its costs are heavily subsidized), or lack of parental engagement in their children's education (even when its returns are very high). These are private behaviors with critical public consequences: overflowing landfills and polluted oceans, overcrowded public hospitals, and a less productive and inequitable society. Governments around the world have experimented with a variety of policies to curb these problems: from taxing products sold in single-use containers, to mandating basic health insurance coverage, to rolling out information campaigns that warn parents about the importance of education. In most cases, such policies have done little to mitigate these problems. This book claims that at least part of the reason is that these policies tend to be designed for an "ideal citizen" who does not really exist out there. Understanding who the "real citizen" is has the potential to unlock opportunities to modify these policies with behavioral insights that could ultimately help us make progress toward these urgent social issues.

This book has three main objectives. First, to incorporate insights from the behavioral sciences and systems thinking in the diagnostics of public problems, based on the motivations and constraints of the "real citizen" – beyond their perfectly rational intentions and plans devoid of social context or self-control problems. Concretely, we introduce a new framework for identifying behavioral constraints that goes far beyond the need for simple reminders and defaults now used by several governments around the world. The second objective is to introduce a new framework for policy design, augmenting commonly used public policy tools with these behavioral insights. The third objective is to condense these insights into a simple toolkit that could be readily used by policy makers or social impact managers faced with complex social challenges. If this book successfully meets these goals, then we will have put scientific evidence and global best practices at the service of citizens.

This book seeks to make cutting-edge theoretical concepts accessible to a general audience, through many examples of how the frameworks we introduce can be applied to real-world problems. Over the course of the different chapters, we focus on issues such as low female labor force participation in Saudi Arabia, low investments in children in Malawi, and low parental engagement in their children's education in Brazil, along with many other examples to illustrate specific behavioral mechanisms, as well as policy innovations augmented by such behavioral insights. While most of the examples we discuss are from low- and middle-income countries (given the authors' backgrounds and expertise), we expect these insights to apply to any policy problem, and this toolkit to be useful even in high-income countries.

We hope that this book serves as an introductory guide to applying behavioral sciences and systems thinking to the day-to-day innovation challenges faced by public sector institutions. In doing so, we hope this work promotes more and better public policies designed for the "real citizen," and that this way of seeing the world – centered on the user, embedded in a complex network of incentives and behavioral constraints – becomes an integral part of every public manager's toolkit.

Palo Alto, CA, USA Guilherme Lichand
São Paulo, Brazil Bruno Rizardi
Brasília, Brazil Amiris de Paula Serdeira

Acknowledgments

This book was inspired by an experimentation project with the Brazilian Government Innovation Lab (GNova), part of the Brazilian National School of Public Administration (ENAP). This work was only possible thanks to the collaboration of many federal public servants who supported the development of these methodologies, and piloted them in real projects targeting wicked social problems – from rural poverty to the engagement of tenured public servants. We acknowledge the contributions of Marizaura Camões, Daniela Gomes Metello, Letícia Mendonça, Márcia Knop, Camila Antonelli, Joselene Lemos, Antonio Claret, Marne Melo, Paula Dias, Ynaia Bueno, Bruno Baranda, Amanda Moreira, Arthur Pomnitz, Bruna Santos, and Guilherme Almeida. We also thank Eppie van Egeraat for helping with translation and proofreading. All remaining errors are ours.

Contents

Chapter 1
Introduction

Do fines really curb habitual drunk driving? Do women demand lower wages when their asks can be seen by colleagues? Do financial incentives discourage parents to follow their children's school life more closely? These questions are motivated by the understanding that citizens do not always exhibit so-called rational (or "ideal") behaviors. Since each of the questions above reflects deeply rooted social problems – behaviors that impose risks on others, gender inequalities, and educational inequalities – understanding which mechanisms influence citizens' "real" behaviors is key to design policies with a real potential to address these problems.

When we think about "ideal" behaviors, we tend to focus on the structural mechanisms behind them: the expected costs and benefits of following different actions, and the extent to which such expectations are accurate. Accordingly, when government intervenes to address such structural mechanisms, it is typically to subsidize costs, to amplify benefits, or to disseminate information about either of those.

In contrast, "real" behaviors might be rooted in very different behavioral mechanisms. People do not always account for all the costs and benefits of their actions. They also often do not make such considerations absent internal conflicts between rationality and affect, or immune from social pressure. Most often than not, they also fail to follow through on past plans – even when those plans looked perfectly rational. This is not how the "ideal" citizen behaves. When government focuses on the "ideal" citizen, it overlooks opportunities to intervene on these alternative mechanisms. What this means is that if, in fact, behavioral mechanisms are an essential part of why people drink and drive, why women might end up being disadvantaged in wage negotiations, or why parents might fail to engage in their children's education, then it might not come as a surprise that these problems are not very responsive to typical governmental interventions.

Electronic Supplementary Material: The online version contains supplementary material available at https://doi.org/10.1007/978-3-031-33034-6_1

G. Lichand et al., *Behavioral Insights for Policy Design*,
https://doi.org/10.1007/978-3-031-33034-6_1

This understanding has only recently entered the universe of policymaking, and even so, very timidly. Hundreds of governments and civil society organizations around the world have come to incorporate some behavioral insights to improve the quality of their programs, especially nudges – changing how information is presented to their target audience in the hope of reallocating their attention or of activating affective considerations towards the "right choice." Most public managers, however, still design policies for the "ideal citizen." Even when they do think of the "real citizen," they often fail to account for the full range of possibilities through which policy tools could be augmented with insights from the behavioral sciences.

Designing policies for the "real citizen" requires understanding what psychological and social mechanisms influence their behaviors, as well as understanding how to enrich policy design to incorporate these mechanisms, to ultimately generate better social outcomes. Developing such understandings is the macro-objective of this book.

This macro-objective can be broken down into four specific objectives. The first is to motivate the inclusion of broader and deeper insights from the behavioral sciences – especially behavioral economics, cognitive psychology, and social psychology – to the repertoire of public managers. The second is to introduce a new methodology for diagnosing public problems – the MSI framework (an acronym for Motivation, Self-control, and Inattention problems) – which will enable us to identify new social problems or reinterpret known problems based on behavioral insights. The third specific objective is to introduce a new methodology for policy design – the PRIx (an acronym for Pricing policies, Regulatory policies, and Information policies) framework – which will enrich existing policy tools with behavioral insights. The fourth specific objective is to offer public managers and all others interested in these issues tools that will allow these methodologies to be applied in a simple and practical way even to complex social problems. A key ingredient to this final objective is the crosscutting application of systems thinking tools, which will help visualize the need for and the potential of interventions with real chances of unlocking persistent changes to the wicked social problems we address throughout the book.

The remainder of the book is organized as follows. Chapter 2 discusses the role of government in accounting for the social costs and benefits of individual actions and in mitigating social inequalities, and expands the motivation for incorporating behavioral insights into policy design. Chapter 3 follows by describing how behavioral insights teams originated and rapidly expanded within the public sector at first, and how they eventually lost steam in face of the need for a new framework. Chapter 4 introduces the MSI framework and explains how to diagnose the most common behavioral mechanisms behind the social problems public managers often have to confront. Chapters 5 and 6 follow by motivating the application of systems thinking tools to complex social problems, and explaining how to embed behavioral insights into those tools. Chapter 7 then introduces the PRIx framework and explains how to augment widely used policy tools with the behavioral insights from the MSI framework. Chapters 8 and 9 follow by providing concrete illustrations for how the MSI-PRIx framework can be used in practice, and collecting best practices and common mistakes in its applications. Chapter 10 then turns to the issue of heterogeneity, and discusses screening and targeting of behavioral types. This is a more advanced chapter, which can be skipped by the reader only seeking an introduction to the topics discussed in this book. Chapter 11 concludes the book with a discussion of lessons learned from the early applications of the MSI-PRIx framework and some perspectives for the future of behavioral or behaviorally informed policy design. We also include a toolkit with supporting materials to guide the reader in applying the MSI-PRIx framework in practice, in Chapter 12. Lecturers and course instructors can find supplementary teaching materials for this book at **http://lichand.info/textbook**.

Summary

1. Government policies typically focus on changing the financial costs or benefits of the behaviors they want to incentivize or discourage, or on informing citizens about these costs and benefits.
2. This is because most public managers design policies for the "ideal citizen" – that who can perfectly process information about the costs and benefits of each action, makes plans based on these inputs in the absence of internal conflicts between reason and affect and immune to social pressure, and always follows through on those plans.
3. In contrast, most people are not like that "ideal citizen." The "real citizen" suffers from motivation, self-control, and inattention problems – which not only render many policies ineffective, but also, often lead to unforeseen distributional consequences.
4. This book explores real citizens' minds, providing practical tools to diagnose plausible behavioral mechanisms behind wicked social problems, and then to augment traditional policy tools with these behavioral insights.
5. Our main goal is that, by designing policies for the "real citizen," policymakers can increase the government's efficacy and equity in addressing those problems.

Chapter 2
Motivating the Use of Behavioral Insights

2.1 New Perspectives for Understanding Social Problems

Among the many roles of government, two are central to its goal of bringing about socially desirable combinations of efficiency and equity. The first is *correcting externalities* – the term economists use to indicate that people or organizations make decisions without fully considering all the costs and benefits that these decisions impose on society. These externalities can be positive or negative. For example, when a driver ingests alcohol and drives while intoxicated, the driver may crash his car or run over a person – imposing a negative externality on society. It would then be the role of the government to define and impose fines[1] and punishments (such as license suspension for drunk driving) because it is assumed that, by doing so, it supports both the task of raising awareness and influencing positive behavior on these drivers, highlighting the social costs of their actions. If successful, the government is able to decrease the undesirable behavior of the driver, who will think twice before drinking and driving, thus decreasing the negative externality.

The second core government function is *inequality reduction* – motivated by views on fairness or by a social contract among its citizens. In the face of social inequalities, it would be up to government to promote socially desirable actions to minimize them. Connected with the example above, government has multiple tools it could use to discourage drunk driving: fines or taxes.[2] Imagine a situation whereby government could achieve the same reduction of the undesirable behavior exclusively through DUI fines, or exclusively through taxes on alcoholic beverages. This would not make the two policy tools equivalent, because each might have very

[1] Fines are defined as a punishment or penalty consisting of a payment (pecuniary sanction). Source: Priberam Online Dictionary. Consulted on 30-11-2021.

[2] Simply put, a tax can be defined as a pecuniary contribution that the state imposes on individuals and legal entities with some legal basis. Source: Priberam Online Dictionary. Consulted on 30-11-2021.

G. Lichand et al., *Behavioral Insights for Policy Design*,
https://doi.org/10.1007/978-3-031-33034-6_2

different impacts on social inequalities. To see that, if alcohol consumption is higher among the poor, but car ownership is higher among the rich, then the burden of fines would be disproportionately borne by the rich, while the tax burden would be disproportionately borne by the poor. All in all, this example makes it clear that the policy mix matters not only for how efficiently externalities can be corrected, but also, for how equitable is the economic incidence of its pecuniary impacts.

When a government imposes fines, bans, and taxes, it bids to change the behavior of its citizens. We expect that more expensive fines, stricter bans, and higher taxes will discourage some behaviors, such as drunk driving. This expectation is based on the so-called rational agent model.

According to the book *Behavioral Sciences and Public Policies*, published by ENAP, in 2020:

"This model, a way of simplifying and abstracting reality to study it within Economics, is based on agents who are able to fully process all available information and make their choices coherently, always aiming to increase their individual welfare.

According to this model, when making a decision, such as buying a car or deciding in which school to enroll their children, people would act in a strictly rational way: they would gather and process all the available information, arrange the options in order of preference according to which would increase their satisfaction, and then choose the best option".

Read more:

> Ciências comportamentais e políticas públicas: o uso do SIMPLES MENTE em projetos de inovação/Antonio Claret Campos Filho; João Sigora; Manuel Bonduki. –Brasília: Enap, 2020.

On the one hand, it is true that, in many cases, people do tend to react as expected by the government when a particular action becomes more expensive. On the other hand, a growing body of scientific evidence documents that human actions are motivated by factors much more complex than the simple monetary costs and benefits of different actions.

Most often than not, government develops policies for what we call the "ideal citizen" – whose decisions are based on perfect cost-benefit calculations, immune to other sources of motivation, to social pressure, and to self-control problems to convert plans into actions. The "ideal citizen" considers only economic incentives: the expected financial benefits and costs associated with each decision, under perfect ability to evaluate these costs and benefits, and to execute decisions perfectly consistent with these plans.

In the real world, the decision-making process is affected by many other factors, which we will call *behavioral mechanisms* (in contrast to the financial costs and benefits, which we will call *structural mechanisms*). Among these factors, we will highlight other sources of motivation, self-control problems, and inattention problems (which motivate the MSI framework that we will cover in this book).

Once these behavioral mechanisms have been understood, we will highlight how commonly used public management tools – pricing policies, regulation, and information policies (which motivate the PRIx framework that we will cover in this book) – can be augmented based on these behavioral insights. In the acronym, the x emphasizes that these tools are used in combination with the behavioral mechanisms from the MSI framework to unlock new possibilities. Ultimately, the MSI-PRIx framework aims at boosting policy instruments already widely used in the public sector, by bringing in new perspectives for the design of public policies centered around the "real citizen."

2.1.1 *Factors that Impact the "Real Citizen"*

One of these factors that condition the behavior of the "real citizen" are other sources of motivation, above and beyond that associated with the financial costs and benefits from his or her actions. *Intrinsic motivation* comes from within and remains relevant even when there is no direct and immediate reward associated with that behavior. Consider, for instance, identity, culture, or religion. This source of motivation induces certain attitudes not because there is a financial reward or punishment associated with them, but because they are connected with what individuals deeply believe to be right or aligned with their values and desires. Extrinsic motivation, in turn, refers to attitudes that are fundamentally driven by factors external to an individual's beliefs and values. Here belong factors such as *social expectations* and *social image* concerns, which condition behaviors through a system of nonfinancial costs and benefits, linked to conformity with the group behavior.

Exemplifying the Types of Motivation

Drivers may be encouraged to drive drunk because they have been raised in a culture that associates self-image with risk-taking, whereby "safer" behaviors are perceived as negative. It would not be surprising if this source of motivation, which we defined above as intrinsic motivation – because it was introjected through culture or education, becoming a value to the individual – made drivers less sensitive to punishment. Drivers can also be stimulated to drive while intoxicated by social pressure from friends gathered around the bar table. This source of motivation, which we call extrinsic motivation – because it is conditioned by the external environment and the situation in which the individual finds him or herself in – also tends to make drivers less sensitive to financial costs associated with breaking the law.

When the government designs fines, taxes, or bans, it is thinking of its "ideal" driver – the rational individual, immune to the influence of these other sources of motivation. The "ideal" driver must not be susceptible to self-image concerns or fall prey to the influences of friends at the bar table! The implication is that traditional public policy tools, such as the fines, taxes, or bans we mentioned above, tend to be far less effective for correcting externalities, considering that drivers are hardly "ideal." The behavior of the "real citizen" depends on a range of behavioral mechanisms, far beyond the monetary costs or benefits of each action.

Another factor that influences human behavior is the ability to exercise self-control. A common phenomenon is that people make ambitious plans to change their behavior in the future, but systematically fail to follow through when that future arrives. Changing plans can be completely rational, especially when we are surprised with new information that we had not anticipated by the time we devised those plans. But when plans are changed systematically, taking place even in the absence of new information, that is indicative of self-control problems. Think about *procrastination*, for example, when we plan to start a new diet or an exercise routine only to keep delaying those plans indefinitely. Self-control problems abound among us, "real citizens" of the world.

Self-control problems are not linked to intentions, but to transforming plans into actions: a driver may arrive at the bar determined not to drink and even commit to being the "designated driver" but end up giving in to *impulsivity* and putting their own life and the lives of others at risk.

Just as in the case of motivation problems, self-control problems also imply low responsivity to fines, taxes, and bans, since the latter reflect precisely the mismatch between intentions (which may be perfectly consistent with rational cost-benefit analysis) and the actual actions, making "real" drivers very different from the "ideal" drivers for whom government designed those policies.

A third behavioral mechanism that conditions human responses above and beyond economic costs and benefits is *inattention*. Since the brain needs to allocate limited energy to its executive functions – attention, working memory, and impulse control – our ability to process stimuli (including information about costs and benefits) is limited.

Back to our example of alcohol consumption, even if the government sets a new tax on alcohol consumption, increasing the costs of this behavior for those who consume it, the individual may not pay attention to the fact that the price has changed on the supermarket shelf and simply continue buying the same amount of cans of beer despite the higher price. In other words, this price increase may not change the citizen's behavior, nor even impact sales. Once again, the "ideal" driver that the government usually has in mind when designing fines, taxes, or bans is often not the one out there. The implication is that traditional public policy tools will tend to be less efficient. Even worse, this example illustrates that ignoring the "real citizen" can also have consequences for equity. Those who ignore higher taxes end up spending more than originally planned (if they continue to purchase the same quantity despite higher prices). Many studies document that inattention tends to hurt the poor disproportionately – because financial worries generate *cognitive load*, "capturing" part of their mental bandwidth. Under cognitive load, less energy is left for the executive functions of the brain, magnifying inattention and the behavioral biases that arise from it. As a result, increasing taxes might not only be ineffective to discourage risky behavior, but also might end up making taxes more regressive – by moving the tax burden to the poor.

2.2 New Perspectives for Designing Public Policies

Typical public policy tools can be organized into three categories. The first public tool is *pricing policies* (taxes, fines, and subsidies fall into this category). Prices potentially affect externalities and equity by affecting the economic costs and/or benefits that condition citizens' decisions. In the examples above, taxes on alcoholic beverages and fines on drunk driving are examples of how the government can utilize pricing policies.

The second public tool is *regulatory policies* (promotion or prohibition of certain conducts fall into this category). When the government makes a behavior compulsory or prohibits it, it utilizes a regulatory policy to correct some externalities, taking equity issues into account.

Examples of Regulatory Policies

When government mandates the use of seat belts, it is trying to influence the behavior of the "ideal citizen" – to reduce the negative externality that he or she imposes on the public health system when they put their own life at risk. Although it may seem that not wearing a seat belt affects only the individual himself, the truth is that all citizens pay taxes that will eventually be used to finance the care of reckless drivers in case of an accident.

Although different in nature, the logic of regulatory policies turns out to be very similar to the one about pricing policies; after all, not following rules is usually associated with financial punishments. If the citizen uses his seat belt to avoid the fine, the policy fulfills its role of reducing negative externalities.

Another example is the ban on smoking in closed environments. By imposing this ban, governments seek to correct negative externalities (due to their impact on the public health system) as well as reduce inequalities, since studies show that the poor tend to smoke more and, therefore, to suffer more health problems resulting from this behavior.

Once again, these policies are typically designed with the "ideal citizen" in mind. As we have seen, for different reasons, the "real citizen" tends to be less responsive to these policies. Given this, it may be that the "real citizen" will not stop smoking cigarettes indoors (or start wearing a seat belt) even with a ban (or a mandate) – even if their decision violates the rational cost-benefit analysis under the regulation in place.

The third typical public policy tool is *information policies* (campaigns fall into this category). Campaigns are typically designed to provide the "ideal citizen" with better information about the economic costs and benefits of their decisions. Ideally, armed with this information, the ideal citizen would then choose the best feasible action. After all, if a citizen only failed to act appropriately due to lack of information, the problem could be easily solved with awareness campaigns. The "real citizen" might be, however, not very responsive to information about financial costs and benefits, either because he or she is inattentive to the campaign or despite of attending to it – because they fail to follow through on the plans that are based on the information it conveys, or because they respond to other sources of motivation instead.

As this discussion makes it clear, designing pricing, regulatory, or information policies with the "ideal citizen" in mind is not the best strategy to come up with instruments able to balance effectiveness and equity in mitigating externalities. Interestingly, the converse is also true: several modern policies that are very effective in changing behavior in the real world do not fit very well into the categories that describe the typical policy tools utilized in the public sector. Concretely, consider policies that try to mitigate school dropouts amongst teenagers. Effective programs to this end tend to mobilize the community, for example, around adolescents' right to education. Community mobilization is not a pricing policy, not a regulatory policy, and not information policy – well, at least not as we described those policies above. Mobilization can be understood as an information policy, but less so because it corrects inaccurate beliefs about the financial costs of early entry into the labor market; rather, because it leverages mechanisms such as social pressure (a key source of extrinsic motivation affecting adolescents' decision to drop out of school). In sum, this strategy is best characterized as an augmented information policy – based on insights from motivation problems.

Now consider instead a conditional cash transfer policy that pays families only if their children attend enough classes throughout the year. But here comes the catch: the program only pays the accumulated amount by the end of the school year. Surprisingly, programs that have this benefit structure tend to have a greater positive impact on educational outcomes for children and youth than those that pay out over time. The reason is that school dropouts are, at least partly, motivated by self-control problems, in face of the temptation to have teenagers enter the job market early to increase family income, at the cost of lowering his or her future income trajectory permanently without a high school diploma. If, on the one hand, disbursements over the course of the school year can help mitigate families' liquidity constraints, on the other hand, the accumulated reward by the end of the school year can help address such self-control problems. Modifying the structure of cash flows from that program to make them less frequent is not a pricing policy, not a regulatory policy, and not information policy – well, at least not as we described those policies above. This strategy is best characterized as an augmented pricing policy – based on insights from self-control problems.

Last, consider a policy that sends weekly text messages to parents of public school students, reminding them of the importance of participating in their children's school life. Programs of this nature are very effective in keeping children in school, attending classes more often, and learning more. Rather than sharing information specific to each student's circumstances, which can be costly or not feasible (especially in low-income settings, in the absence of electronic systems to track student attendance, assignments, and grades at high frequency), the program tries to merely reallocate parents' attention, inducing them monitor each student on their own. Reallocating attention to induce independent information acquisition is not a pricing policy, not a regulatory policy, and not an information policy – well, at least not as we described those policies above. This strategy is best characterized as an augmented information policy – based on insights from inattention problems.

The examples above suggest that the effectiveness of these policies could be boosted even more by combining different behavioral mechanisms with each policy tool. For instance, community mobilization could also be used to mitigate limiting mental models (in this case, to prevent parents from pulling their children from school), or to increase parents' attention to the costs of dropping out. In turn, the cash transfer program could be combined with strategies to reinforce parents' and students' motivation to stay in school. Moreover, the text messaging program could be combined with other approaches, for example, leveraging social pressure of peers who want to remain in school, or developing self-regulation skills to make children and adolescents better able to resist the temptations of immediate gratification. The possibilities are endless!

The next chapters deepen the discussion of how to identify behavioral mechanisms behind complex social problems, through the MSI framework, and how to augment public policy tools based on these behavioral insights, through the PRIx framework.

But, before that, we turn to the early days of the applications of behavioral insights in the public sector, to understand how they started and how they eventually reached important limitations – for it is precisely those limitations that call for the new framework that we offer in this book.

Summary

1. Governments have two central roles in society: correcting externalities and reducing social inequalities. To achieve these goals, governments have various policy tools at their disposal; such as fines, bans, and information campaigns.
2. These strategies are typically modeled on an ideal citizen. None of us, however, behaves according to that ideal model.
3. There are several factors that affect the behaviors of the real citizen, such as motivation, self-control, and inattention problems.
4. As such, there are many ways to leverage behavioral insights to design better social programs. In fact, some of the most effective policies incorporate these mechanisms – and it might not be easy to understand or to influence citizens' behaviors without them.
5. Traditional policy tools can typically be organized into three categories: prices, which include taxes, fines, and subsidies; regulation, which includes mandates and bans; and information, which includes campaigns.
6. Understanding these mechanisms and tools opens a new world of possibilities for designing public policies informed by behavioral insights.

Suggested Readings

BENKERT, Jean-Michel, and Nick NETZER (2018a) "Informational Requirements of Nudging," Journal of Political Economy, 126(6), pp. 2323– 2355.

CHETTY, Raj, Adam LOONEY, and Kory KROFT (2009a) "Salience and Taxation: Theory and Evidence", The American Economic Review, 99(4), pp. 1145–77.

DELLAVIGNA, Stefano, and Elizabeth LINOS (2020a) "RCTs to Scale: Comprehensive Evidence from Two Nudge Units," NBER Working Paper No. 27594, July 2020.

JOHNSON, Eric, and Daniel GOLDSTEIN (2003a) "Do Defaults Save Lives?", Science, 302(5649), pp. 1338–1339.

LICHAND, Guilherme, Eric BETTINGER, Nina CUNHA, and Ricardo MADEIRA (2020a) "The Psychological Effects of Poverty on Investments in Children's Human Capital," available at SSRN: https://ssrn.com/abstract=3644127.

ALAN, Sule; BONEVA, Teodora; ERTAC, Seda. Ever failed, try again, succeed better: results from a randomized education on grit. The Quarterly Jouvenal of Economics, 134, 3, p. 1121–1161, 2019, Available at: https://bit.ly/3Wm8uCQ.

MANI, Anandi, Sendhil MULLAINATHAN, Eldar SHAFIR, and Jiaying ZHAO (2013a) "Poverty Impedes Cognitive Function", Science, 341(6149), pp. 976–980.

SHAFIR, Eldar and Sendhil MULLAINATHAN (2013a) "Scarcity: Why Having Too Little Means So Much", Times Books.

SHAH, Anuj K, Sendhil MULLAINATHAN, and Eldar SHAFIR (2012a) "Some Consequences of Having Too Little", Science, 338(6107), pp. 682– 685.

SHAH, Anuj K, Eldar SHAFIR, and Sendhil MULLAINATHAN (2015a) "Scarcity Frames Value", Psychological Science, 26(4), pp. 402–412.

WOODFORD, Michael (2020a) "Modeling Imprecision in Perception, Valuation, and Choice", Annual Review of Economics, 12, pp. 579–601.

Behavioral Sciences and Public Policies: the use of SIMPLE MIND in innovation projects (GNOVA, 2020)

BURSZTYN, Leonardo, Thomas FUJIWARA, and Amanda PALLAIS (2017) "'Acting Wife': Marriage Market Incentives and Labor Market Investments," The American Economic Review, 107(11), pp. 3288–3319.

BURSZTYN, Leonardo, Alessandra GONZALES, and David YANAGIZAWA-DROTT (2020) "Misperceived Social Norms: Female Labor Force Participation in Saudi Arabia," The American Economic Review, 110(10), pp. 2997–3029.

CURRARINI, Sergio, and Friederike MENGEL (2016) "Identity, Homophily and In-group Bias", European Economic Review, 90, pp. 40–55.

FRACCHIA, Mattia, Teresa MOLINA, and Pedro VICENTE (2019) "Incentivizing Community Health Workers in Guinea-Bissau: Experimental Evidence on Social Status and Intrinsic Motivation", mimeo.

FRYER, Roland, and Paul TORELLI (2010) "An Empirical Analysis of 'Acting White'", Journal of Public Economics, 94(5–6), 380–396.

HAENNI, Simon, and Guilherme LICHAND (2021) "Harming to Signal: Child Marriage Vs. Public Donations in Malawi", Available at SSRN: https://ssrn.com/abstract=3633803.

KARING, Anne (2021) "Social Signaling and Childhood Immunization: A Field Experiment in Sierra Leone", mimeo.

LICHAND, Guilherme, and Sharon WOLF (2021) "Arm-Wrestling in the Classroom: The Non-Monotonic Effects of Monitoring Teachers," available at SSRN: https://ssrn.com/abstract=3662146.

CASABURI, Lorenzo, and Jack WILLIS (2018) "Time Vs. State Insurance: Experimental Evidence From Contract Farming in Kenya", The American Economic Review, 108(2), pp. 3778–3813.

CLARO, Susana, David PAUNESKU, and Carol S. DWECK (2016) "Growth Mindset Tempers the Effects of Poverty on Academic Achievement." PNAS, 113(31), pp. 8664–8668.

DIZON-ROSS, Rebecca, and Ariel ZUCKER (2021) "Can Price Discrimination Incentivize Behavior Change? Evidence From a Randomized Field Experiment," mimeo.
DUFLO, Esther, Michael KREMER, and Jonathan ROBINSON (2011) "Nudging Farmers to Use Fertilizer: Theory and Experimental Evidence from Kenya", The American Economic Review, 101(6), pp. 2350–90.
DUQUENNOIS, Claire (2021) "Fictional Money, Real Costs: Impacts of Financial Salience on Disadvantaged Students," mimeo. HAUSHOFER, Johannes, and Ernst FEHR (2014) "On The Psychology of Poverty", Science, 344(6186), pp. 862–867.
HELLER, Sara, Harold POLLACK, Roseanna ANDER, and Jens LUDWIG (2013) "Preventing Youth Violence and Dropout: A Randomized Field Experiment," NBER Working Paper No. 19014, May 2013.
JOB, Veronika, Carol S. DWECK, and Gregory WALTON (2010) "Ego Depletion – Is It All In Your Head? Implicit Theories About Willpower Affect Self-Regulation," Psychological Science, 21(11), pp. 1686–93.
LICHAND, Guilherme, and Juliette THIBAUD (2020) "Parent-Bias", Available at SSRN: https://ssrn.com/abstract=3737685.
SCHILBACH, Frank (2019) "Alcohol and Self-Control: A Field Experiment in India," The American Economic Review, 109(4), pp. 1290–1322.
SHAH, Anuj K, Sendhil MULLAINATHAN, and Eldar SHAFIR (2012b) "Some Consequences of Having Too Little", Science, 338(6107), pp. 682–685.
SHIV, Baba, and Alexander FEDORIKHIN (1999) "Heart and Mind in Conflict: The Interplay of Affect and Cognition in Consumer Decision Making", Journal of Consumer Research, 26(3), pp. 278–292.
YEAGER, David S, Paul HANSELMAN, Gregory M. WALTON, Jared S. MURRAY, Robert CROSNOE, Chandra MULLER, Elizabeth TIPTON, Barbara SCHNEIDER, Chris S. HULLEMAN, Cintia P. HINOJOSA, David PAUNESKU, Carissa ROMERO, Kate FLINT, Alice ROBERTS, Jill TROTT, Ronaldo IACHAN, Jenny BUONTEMPO, Sophia Man YANG, Carlos M. CARVALHO, P. Richard HAHN, Maithreyi GOPALAN, Pratik MHATRE, Ronald FERGUSON, Angela L. DUCKWORTH, and Carol S. DWECK (2019) "A National Experiment Reveals Where a Growth Mindset Improves Achievement," Nature, 573, pp. 364–369.
BENKERT, Jean-Michel, and Nick NETZER (2018b) "Informational Requirements of Nudging," Journal of Political Economy, 126(6), pp. 2323–2355.
CHETTY, Raj, Adam LOONEY, and Kory KROFT (2009b) "Salience and Taxation: Theory and Evidence", The American Economic Review, 99(4), pp. 1145–77.
DELLAVIGNA, Stefano, and Elizabeth LINOS (2020b) "RCTs to Scale: Comprehensive Evidence from Two Nudge Units," NBER Working Paper No. 27594, July 2020.
JOHNSON, Eric, and Daniel GOLDSTEIN (2003b) "Do Defaults Save Lives?", Science, 302(5649), pp. 1338–1339.
LICHAND, Guilherme, Eric BETTINGER, Nina CUNHA, and Ricardo MADEIRA (2020b) "The Psychological Effects of Poverty on Investments in Children's Human Capital," available at SSRN: https://ssrn.com/abstract=3644127.
MANI, Anandi, Sendhil MULLAINATHAN, Eldar SHAFIR, and Jiaying ZHAO (2013b) "Poverty Impedes Cognitive Function", Science, 341(6149), pp. 976–980.
Shafir, Eldar and Sendhil MULLAINATHAN (2013b) "Scarcity: Why Having Too Little Means So Much", Times Books.
SHAH, Anuj K, Sendhil MULLAINATHAN, and Eldar SHAFIR (2012c) "Some Consequences of Having Too Little", Science, 338(6107), pp. 682–685.
SHAH, Anuj K, Eldar SHAFIR, and Sendhil MULLAINATHAN (2015b) "Scarcity Frames Value", Psychological Science, 26(4), pp. 402–412.
WOODFORD, Michael (2020b) "Modeling Imprecision in Perception, Valuation, and Choice", Annual Review of Economics, 12, pp. 579–601

Chapter 3
The Rise and the Fall of Governmental Nudge Units

3.1 Choice Architecture, Nudges, and Libertarian Paternalism

As discussed, the real citizen does not approach decisions purely based on a rational computation of its expected costs and benefits. In particular, she is often not fully attentive to the trade-offs involved in the problem at hand. With that in mind, it might be unsurprising that the details of how decisions are framed can be hugely influential on what the real citizen ultimately chooses – even if the structural aspects of the problem remain unchanged across different framings. Concretely, in our example of habitual drunk driving, the sensitivity of consumers to price changes of alcoholic beverages will typically depend on how easy one can visualize those changes upon casually inspecting the menu – in technical terms, on how salient the price change is.

The cognitive psychology metaphor for how the elements of choice might ultimately influence its outcome is that of a choice architecture. It is like subjects enter a building with many different elements whenever they make a decision. Some elements might be hidden behind columns, some might be easier to spot. Those that are more visible have a higher likelihood of being accounted for.

There is substantial evidence that this metaphor has empirical bite. One of its most well-known examples is how default options seem to change the decision to donate organs dramatically. A study compared the ratio of drivers who opted to have their organs donated in case of a fatal accident across several countries. While Austria, Belgium, France, Hungary, Poland, and Portugal had nearly 100% of drivers agree to donate their organs, that rate was only 27.5% in the Netherlands, 17% in the UK, 12% in Germany, and 4.3% in Denmark. What was the source of such striking differences? Researchers found that the main difference was that while the latter set of countries required explicit consent – that is, each individual had to actively opt in to become a donor – the former set only required presumed consent,

G. Lichand et al., *Behavioral Insights for Policy Design*,
https://doi.org/10.1007/978-3-031-33034-6_3

that is, each individual was made an organ donor by default, and had to actively opt out in case they did not want to.

If that metaphor has explanatory power, it invites intervention – especially in the domain of problems that have public consequences, from externalities to social inequalities. The term *nudge* was coined to represent changes to the choice architecture, even if slight, with the goal of moving the choice of the real citizen closer to that of the ideal citizen. Interestingly, that can be done in two ways that can be thought of as complete opposites. First, by trying to *circumvent* inattention, increasing the salience of the essential elements of the problem (its expected costs and benefits). The amounts to reframing the problem, highlighting these elements, and/or removing other, nonessential elements, in order to move the inputs for rational decision-making onto the spotlight. Second, by trying to *leverage* inattention, playing out the exact same tendencies of the real citizen to overlook essential elements of the problem at hand but to induce her to choose what the ideal citizen would even in the absence of a rational computation of its costs and benefits. Concretely, an example of the first strategy is highlighting price increases of alcoholic beverages in red and with larger font size in the bar menu. Examples of the second strategy are moving alcoholic beverages to the very end of the menu or setting nonalcoholic drinks as the default option whenever someone orders a beer.

Such strategies have proven extremely seductive for public sector managers worldwide, for two main reasons. First, because in many applications they seem to bear nearly zero costs, with a potential to deliver better outcomes. Consider a public campaign to discourage drunk driving that was already set to go to print. Reframing the campaign to target behavioral biases of the real citizen might have low or even no costs in some cases, with some higher potential of changing his or her behavior relative to a purely informational piece that fails to account for inattention and salience.

Second, because of a long-standing and very much alive debate on what is the role of government, particularly when it comes to shaping individual decisions towards social goals. On the one hand, some believe citizens often make bad decisions for society (because of externalities) and even for themselves (especially amongst the poor, e.g., because of limited access to education). In principle, that justifies government paternalism: imposing certain decisions, through prohibitions or mandates, that are desirable for society. A common example is schooling, which is mandatory in many societies around the world. In those societies, the social contract does not lend to individuals the agency to make decisions of whether or not their children should be educated based on computations of the expected costs and benefits of attending school for longer. Education is a paternalistic (often constitutional) mandate. On the other hand, some believe only each person knows what is best for him or herself. In principle, that justifies libertarianism: preventing governmental interference in individual choice in as many domains as possible. A common example is organ donations upon death, which is a purely individual choice in most societies around the world.

Nudges defy that dichotomy. The intention behind changing the salience of certain elements of the decision problem, or defaulting a different option, is to shape individual choice. This makes nudges consistent with paternalism. At the same time, changing the choice architecture preserves freedom of choice; after all, individuals are still free to pick the very same choice under alternative framings. As such, nudges are also consistent with libertarianism. For this reason, that approach to public policy became known as libertarian paternalism.

Cost-effectiveness and libertarian paternalism fueled the adoption of nudges in the public sector, first in high-income countries like the UK, and later in middle- and low-income countries worldwide.

3.2 Nudges in the Public Sector: How It Started Versus How It Is Going

In 2010, The UK created the world's first Nudge Unit (later rebranded as Behavioral Insights Team). Established in the Cabinet Office by David Cameron's government, its goal was to apply behavioral insights to public policy.

This teamwork was cross-sectorial, collaborating closely with public sector managers across economic, health, educational, and environmental topics. Several of the innovative approaches they codesigned were rigorously evaluated and eventually scaled up, benefitting the universe of UK citizens. The team helped simplify complex information about pension plans, condensing 50+ pages of information into a single sheet; visits to the advice website increased by a factor of 10. They helped raise awareness about the importance of recycling through a campaign that changed the color of the bins, increasing demand for composting by up to 60%. They also codesigned a simpler sign-up form for NHS patients, whereby fewer data sharing options led to a near fourfold increase in patients opting in to share data, improving the ability to monitor and predict aggregate health conditions.

The US government followed suit in 2015, with its Office of Evaluation Sciences. Nudges units spread rapidly ever since, including to middle- and low-income countries. As of 2023, over 200 such units had been identified by the OECD.

These teams were typically focused on quick wins: identifying light-touch interventions informed by behavioral insights that could increase the take-up of desirable behaviors at no or low cost. That often meant modifying the choice architecture by reframing decisions: simplifying information, recasting details of the problem at hand, and changing default options, as the examples we discussed help illustrate.

Such global expansion was boosted not only by the leading examples of the UK and the USA in paving the way for the applications of new policy tools informed by insights from cognitive psychology, but also by a rapidly growing evidence base that showed that the impacts of nudge interventions could be, somewhat surprisingly, extremely large. A study published in 2009 found that compelling new hires to make active decisions about pension enrollment in the USA increased the share of enrollees by 60% relative to a standard opt-in enrollment procedure. Another study published in 2012 found that simplifying financial aid information for low-income college students more than doubled the share of eligible individuals who submitted the aid application, enrolled in college the following fall, and ultimately received more financial aid. As a final example, a study published in 2013 found that changing the menu order in a college cafeteria buffet line led the percentage of students making healthier meal choices by nearly 50%.

Although on the high end of effect sizes published in scientific journals, these examples are not isolated cases. A meta-analysis published in 2022 found that the average effect size of nudges on binary decisions published in academic journals, documented through randomized control trials – whereby nudges are assigned to a "treatment" group, which is then compared to a "control" group not targeted by nudges, with assignment determined by lottery – to be about one-third of the baseline take-up. This is a huge return to a policy that, as discussed, could often be implemented at a very low cost.

Outside of the university halls, however, the story was a lot less shiny, for two main reasons. First, nudge units were typically not reaching the same level of success as the interventions evaluated in the studies published by academic journals. As that meta-analysis shows, most interventions actually did not work at all, with an average effect size of only ~8% (only about one-fourth of the average one in published scientific papers). Concretely, that often meant boosting take-up of desirable behaviors from 20% to 21.4% – a very modest increase. Second, even when these interventions worked, they were often not scaled up by the government. A working paper published in 2022 found that only 27% of nudge-like interventions rigorously evaluated by local US governments in partnership with a national nudge unit were subsequently adopted.

All in all, the initial excitement for the application of nudges in the public sector eventually lost steam. Despite their low costs, nudges did not really transform the take-up of public services or desirable behaviors as expected. Where did things go wrong?

3.3 The Need for a New Framework

The potential reasons for why the typical effects of nudge-like interventions ran by nudge units did not match those published in scientific papers are likely manyfold. A leading one is that scientific journals display a known tendency to disproportionately publish positive results. This means successful interventions will be overrepresented in academic journals. Since nudge units do not suffer from the same tendency, it might just be that published scientific papers are a selected sample of the "true effects" of these interventions. In other words, the typical effect of nudges might indeed be much lower if we were able to see the results of every study ever conducted – even if their results were fluke.

There are, of course, other reasons. Nudge units are often unable to experiment with changing default options, which are typically the interventions with the largest impacts on individual choice. Moreover, nudge units often have to move more quickly and with less room for piloting and adaptative experimentation than scientists. While we can rationalize this difference in multiple ways, what matters is that the interventions' nudge units are typically able to implement, and how they do it, most often than not lead to disappointing impacts. This suggests that successful interventions for the real citizen must produce large impacts within the constraints of what governments can typically execute.

Interestingly, this is not the only reason for why these interventions are often not scaled up even when successful. Governments are complex organizations. The 2022 study found that the few interventions that eventually scaled were the ones that had already been in place, piloted before the evaluation. This is likely because such interventions already had political buy-in. In contrast, new interventions, even when informed by external success and with locally validated impacts, still have to go the extra mile of being championed by public managers willing to invest their political capital in promoting them – which takes both capacity to influence and time. This suggests that behaviorally informed interventions with a real potential to scale up and eventually benefit all citizens must ideally operate within the boundaries of existing policy tools that public managers already have at their disposal.

Drawing from a larger set of behavioral insights – not only from cognitive psychology, but also from social psychology, social anthropology, and beyond – and embedding them in *existing policy tools* requires a new framework, which is the object of this book.

Naturally, nudge units started changing over time in response to perceptions that they did not live up to their original promise. The most common reaction was to start looking beyond inattention, at other potential light-touch interventions informed by behavioral insights that could potentially unlock larger impacts on citizen behavior.

Remember that real citizens are not just often inattentive to the details of the decision at hand, but also often vulnerable to internal affective conflicts and social pressure. A common set of interventions that quickly spreads across these behavioral insights teams was communication to dispel inaccurate social expectations. Consider the example of adolescents deciding whether to drop out of school in middle- and low-income countries. Part of the reason behind dropouts might be incorrect beliefs that most peers are unmotivated to remain in school, even if most of them would actually prefer to do so (but do not openly say so). Often, such interventions take the form of surveying a representative sample of the target population to elicit credible information about the behavior of interest, and then sharing that information with the target population more broadly.

Examples abound. In 2015, the UK Behavioral Insights Team tested whether leveraging social expectations in communications from mortgage lenders increased callbacks from mortgagers in financial distress. In 2017, they tested whether comparing one's energy consumption to that of their neighbors effectively led consumers to save energy, leveraging social expectations and social image concerns. In 2019, the team tried to reduce NHS doctors' overprescription of antibiotics by contrasting their prescribing behavior to that of their peers.

As we will discuss in the next chapters, while motivation problems are indeed a fruitful avenue for behaviorally informed policies, there are many other possibilities, and different problems might require different approaches, or even a combination of levers targeting both behavioral and structural mechanisms. Without an integrated framework, such a piecemeal approach is unlikely to produce systematically large impacts. In effect, such changes did not reignite the initial flame of nudge units in the most recent years. Most importantly, as our previous discussion highlights, such an approach is not really integrated with the policy tools available for public managers in their day-to-day activities. Nudge units often pitch their work as offering tools that public managers had never considered. While that pitch might be effective in catching the eye, there is good reason to believe that it contains its own demise, as even successful out-of-the-box interventions are unlikely to scale when there is no initial political buy-in. In contrast, the next chapters will also discuss how such insights can be successfully integrated into policy instruments already in place.

Summary

1. As discussed, the real citizen does not approach decisions purely based on a rational computation of its expected costs and benefits. As such, their decisions are often influenced by how such decisions are framed (the choice architecture).
2. The details of how decisions are framed can be surprisingly influential on what the real citizen ultimately chooses even if the structural aspects of the problem remain unchanged across different framings. One of its most well-known examples is how default options seem to change the decision to donate organs dramatically.
3. Often, governments try to improve outcomes with only small changes to how decisions are framed. The term **nudge** was coined to represent changes to the choice architecture, even if slight, with the goal of moving the choice of the real citizen closer to that of the ideal citizen. Interestingly, that can be done in two ways that can be thought of as complete opposites: (1) highlighting incentives, increasing their salience in an attempt to approximate the ideal citizen's *optimal* decision process, or (2) downplaying undesirable alternatives, decreasing their salience in an attempt to leverage the real citizen's *constrained* decision process.
4. Such strategies have proven extremely seductive for public sector managers worldwide, first, because in many applications they seem to bear nearly zero costs, with a potential to deliver better outcomes; second, because of a long-standing and very much alive debate on what is the role of government, particularly when it comes to shaping individual decisions towards social goals.
5. As this approach might preserve not only free choice but also create small incentives for behavior adjustments, it became known as libertarian paternalism.
6. Cost-effectiveness and libertarian paternalism fueled the adoption of nudges in the public sector, first in high-income countries like the UK, and later in middle- and low-income countries worldwide.

7. Although scientifically exciting, as it turns out, nudges were more effective on academic papers than outside of the classroom walls. Worse, even when effective, policies informed by behavioral insights were often not scaled up.
8. Naturally, nudge units started changing over time in response to perceptions that they did not live up to their original promise. But their typical piece-meal approach and the lack of integration with existing policies ultimately made them lose their initial steam. The next chapters discuss how such insights can be broadened to account for a more comprehensive set of behavioral mechanisms and successfully integrated into policy instruments already in place.

Suggested Readings

Thaler, R. H., & Sunstein, C. R. (2008). Nudge: Improving decisions about health, wealth, and happiness. Yale University Press.

Behavioral Insights Team. 2020, Accessed 30 January 2023, https://www.bi.team/.

Stefano DellaVigna & Elizabeth Linos, 2022. "RCTs to Scale: Comprehensive Evidence From Two Nudge Units," Econometrica, Econometric Society, vol. 90(1), pages 81-116.

Stefano DellaVigna & Woojin Kim & Elizabeth Linos, 2022. "Bottlenecks for Evidence Adoption," NBER Working Papers 30144, National Bureau of Economic Research, Inc.

Chapter 4
Diagnosing Behavioral Mechanisms Behind Public Problems: The MSI Framework

4.1 Introduction

This chapter presents a novel methodology for diagnosing policy-relevant behavioral mechanisms: the *MSI framework* – whereby the acronym stands for motivation, self-control, and inattention problems. This framework is informed by the behavioral sciences, particularly economics, cognitive psychology, and social psychology.

These disciplines recognize that individuals respond to a range of incentives, not only financial. As we saw earlier, public policies designed for the "ideal citizen" typically consider only economic incentives – that is, the expected financial benefits and costs associated with each decision. They also usually assume that citizens make plans with a perfect capacity to evaluate these costs and benefits, and that he or she is able to execute decisions which are perfectly consistent with these plans over time.

In contrast, the MSI framework considers the mechanisms that mediate the decision-making process of the "real citizen." In addition to economic incentives, this citizen is motivated by many other factors. In Section 4.2, we will discuss the sources and implications of real citizens' motivations above and beyond financial incentives: *intrinsic motivation* (which include identity, culture, and religion) and *extrinsic motivation* (social pressure and social image concerns). In Section 4.3, we will discuss the sources and implications of real citizen's self-control problems: *impulsivity, procrastination,* and *limiting mental models* – all associated with intertemporal inconsistencies between plans and actions. Last, in Section 4.4, we will discuss the sources and implications of real citizen's inattention problems: *cognitive biases*, associated with systematic errors in decision-making, especially in the presence of *cognitive load* (external conditions that impose additional demands on citizen's mental bandwidth, such as poverty-induced financial worries), and *learning through noticing* (when they disregard essential features of the environment even when information is available at low cost).

G. Lichand et al., *Behavioral Insights for Policy Design*,
https://doi.org/10.1007/978-3-031-33034-6_4

The MSI framework leaves out some behavioral mechanisms widely studied by some of these sciences. In particular, our framework does not focus on risk preferences[1] or social preferences (such as altruism or reciprocity, which might account for economic incentives that affect others, rather than oneself). This methodological choice and its limitations will be discussed in Section 4.5.

4.2 Motivation Problems

Next, we will discuss the sources and implications of real citizens'motivations beyond the financial costs and benefits of their actions.

4.2.1 Intrinsic Motivation: Identity, Culture, and Religion

Several studies document that certain sources of motivation lead individuals to make decisions contrary to the logic dictated by financial costs and benefits, even when these decisions are not observable to anyone else. People tend to avoid decisions that conflict with their values and their perceptions about themselves, and to make decisions that confirm these values and perceptions.

For instance, a person may decide to help someone anonymously, without expecting anything in return, because he or she is intrinsically motivated to help others. This individual may have this attitude because of aspects of their upbringing that make them see charity as part of their identity, or because of their religion. Some of these "triggers" might be quite subtle: perhaps he or she grew up with a grandmother who was actively engaged in charitable causes, which led them to impersonate that trait as part of their identity.

At the other extreme, an individual may decide to use corporal punishment as a disciplinary strategy in the upbringing of his or her children, or to put their children to work even if the family's economic standing does not require having to sacrifice time from their studies, in order to replicate aspects of their culture or upbringing that they consider to be part of their identity (e.g., because their parents also did this to them).

One interesting behavioral bias that can be linked to intrinsic motivation is what scientists call cognitive dissonance. This is the tendency to overlook information that contradicts one's actions or beliefs, to preserve a sense of continuity or

[1] This occurs when the individual exhibits reluctance to accept a deal with an uncertain return, rather than another deal with a more certain but possibly lower expected return. This mechanism has implications for the demand for insurance, for example, since this product is useful for preventing losses, but only makes sense when the buyer is risk-averse.

consistency with their internal belief system. Cognitive dissonance helps explain why we tend to seek information that confirms what we already believe in, and might be behind the increasing polarization we see in media consumption and political views.

Intrinsic motivations are typically difficult to change. Imagine trying to change motivational factors intimately tied to a culture or religion? That said, recognizing that these elements are present in real citizens'decision-making can create opportunities to intervene in public policy design. This is because reinforcing or minimizing aspects of identity, culture, or religion in the way we motivate a policy (in particular, what elements we highlight when we announce which target audience it is aimed at) can be a powerful driver for reinforcing or discouraging certain behaviors (see Fig. 4.1).

4.2.2 Social Expectations

A number of studies document that individuals are sensitive to social punishments and rewards, even when their financial implications are not clear. Typically, such social incentives are linked to conformity to the behavior of the social group in which the individual is embedded, either because the behavior in question is valued (in the case of incentives) or because it is rejected (in the case of punishments) by the group. Social incentives get stronger the more the citizen cares about what other group members think of them, the more visible the behavior is to the group, and the more strongly a behavior serves as a social signal for other attributes that are more difficult to observe (see Fig. 4.2).

An example of this is social recognition. Research shows that, in certain sub-Saharan African countries, community health agents put more effort into their functions when they think that their work is recognized by the families they serve.

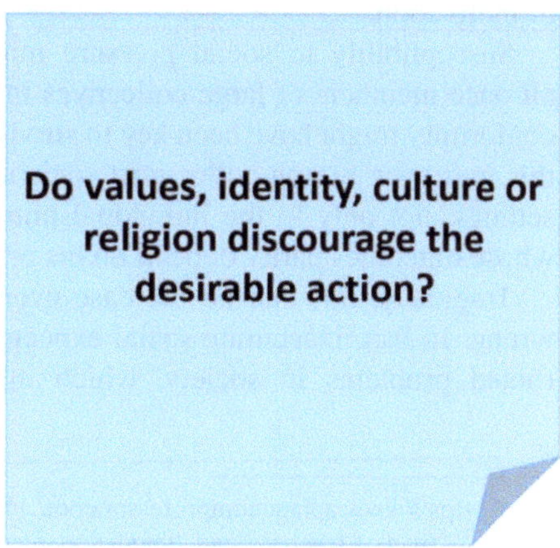

Fig. 4.1 Intrinsic motivation. (Source: Provided by the Authors)

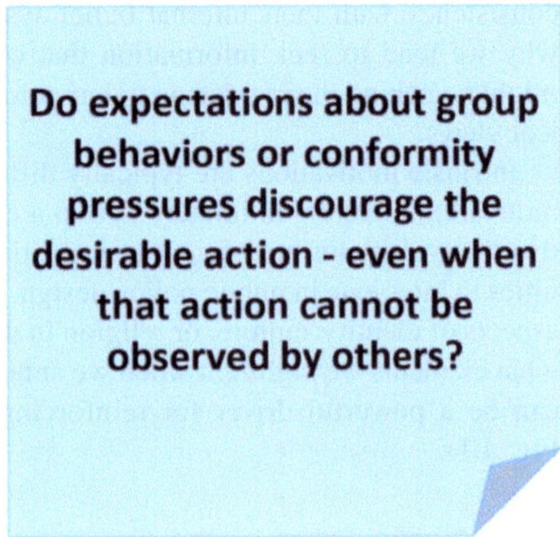

Fig. 4.2 Social expectations. (Source: Provided by the Authors)

A Brazilian parallel to this was the "Applaud a teacher" campaign,[2] modeled after the idea that teachers put in more effort when their work is publicly appreciated.

Social punishments can also induce behaviors with public consequences. For instance, parents make an effort to pick up their children early from day care partly because they do not want to be perceived as bad parents by caregivers – even if they do not interact with these caregivers in any other setting that would justify social image concerns (which we will address in the next section).

Interestingly, when Israeli day care centers introduced fines to financially punish tardy parents, the frequency and length of tardiness actually increased! The likely reason is that the fine "put a price" on guilt – parents understood the charge as if it were a payment for overtime. In other words, the social punishment of "forgetting the child" was more powerful than the financial punishment of being fined for lateness, at least in this context and for the amount of the fine set by day care centers.

It is not so difficult to activate extrinsic motivation mechanisms in the design of public policies. As the example above makes it clear, the "real citizen" usually tries to infer the reasons why policies or rules were designed, and reacts to these sources of motivation.

Susceptibility to social pressure might have evolutionary roots, as we were all once members of large collectives in times of scarcity, when collaboration and conformity might have been key to survival. Nowadays, however, the persistence of this trait even in non-collectivist societies might come with large costs – in some settings, not only to the individual him or herself, but also, potentially to others whose outcomes partly depend on his or her decisions.

Tragically, this can be the case even when social expectations are ultimately wrong. In fact, inaccurate social expectations are behind some of the most deeply rooted problems in society, which might not seem very amenable to public

[2] See https://www.aplaudaumprofessor.com/. Similar initiatives are the campaigns "honor a teacher," "thank a teacher," and "thank you, teacher."

intervention. The box discusses the striking example of how misperceptions about men's support for female labor force participation in Saudi Arabia keep most wives from looking for jobs. While this is challenging, we will discuss in the next chapter how this also provides opportunities to intervene.

Female Labor Force Participation in Saudi Arabia

In Saudi Arabia, a study documented that most husbands do not privately object to their wives working. However, most men are unaware that this is the case: the typical husband believes he is one of the few who thinks this way. Out of conformity pressures, and in response to these inaccurate social expectations, most men do not allow their wives to seek work even though this contradicts their personal beliefs (Bursztyn et al. 2018).

Saudi husbands tend to overestimate the proportion of other men who object to women's participation in the labor market by a large margin.

Read more:

BURSZTYN, Leonardo, Alessandra GONZALES, and David YANAGIZAWA-DROTT (2020) "Misperceived Social Norms: Female Labor Force Participation in Saudi Arabia", The American Economic Review, 110(10), pp. 2997–3029.

4.2.3 Social Image Concerns

There is clear evidence that individuals respond to social pressure, especially when their actions are visible to other individuals with whom they frequently interact (see Fig. 4.3). Human beings seem to have a natural tendency to form groups, and to treat those who are (or are not) part of them differently. This includes the so-called

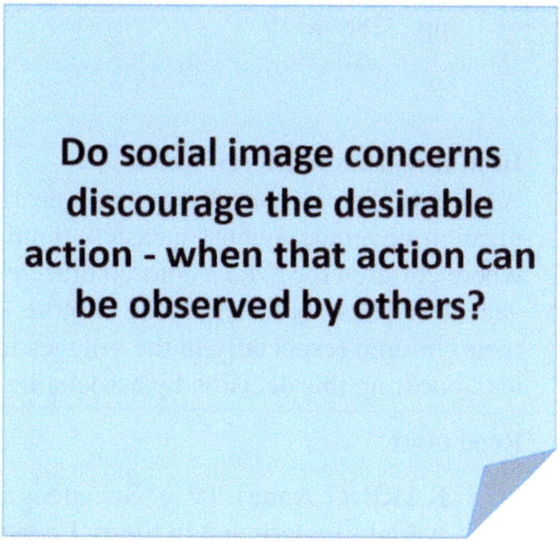

Fig. 4.3 Social image concerns. (Source: Provided by the Authors)

herd behavior: adopting certain behaviors for no good reason other than following in-group members, or in opposition to behaviors of out-group members.

In many cases, individuals may yield to social pressure even when the expected cost of the action is high (at least in financial terms). A study in the United States found that high school students of color did not put effort towards very good grades in order not to look like other social groups – white students, with a higher GPA – whom they did not want to identify with.

In face of social image concerns, the extent to which an action is visible might completely change the behavior of some individuals. Consistent with this mechanism, the share of students of color enrolled in advanced placement (AP) courses in that US study increased when the "honor roll" with those enrolled in AP courses was no longer publicly displayed in the school.

Gender Salary "Ask Gap" in the United States

A study with Master of Business Administration (MBA) students at the University of Chicago documented that single female students had lower class participation scores relative to married women or male students (single or married), even though there was no difference in their proficiency on written tests. The study used an experiment to show that the salary ask by these female students was much lower than that of their classmates – but only if they knew that their ask could be observed by their peers.

Researchers further showed that this behavior is closely linked to concerns about not being perceived by their colleagues as too ambitious or work-oriented. Results make it clear that the actions of certain individuals can change drastically not only in response to social expectations, but also to the visibility of their actions.

Read more:

BURSZTYN, Leonardo, Thomas FUJIWARA, and Amanda PALLAIS (2017) "'Acting Wife': Marriage Market Incentives and Labor Market Investments", The American Economic Review, 107(11), pp. 3288–3319.

Immunization in Sierra Leone

A study in Sierra Leone documents a nearly 30% increase in the rate of immunization coverage against measles, mumps, and rubella (MMR) in villages where children received a colored bracelet if they had taken the full course of vaccines. These bracelets made it more visible that parents had immunized their children (especially in the villages farthest from the immunization clinics), boosting this decision by associating it with parents' social image.

Read more:

KARING, Anne (2021) "Social Signaling and Childhood Immunization: A Field Experiment in Sierra Leone," mimeo.

Child Marriage in Malawi

A study in Malawi shows that many parents marry off their daughters before they turn 18 years old (the minimum legal age in the country) despite privately opposing the practice. The study documents that this happens, at least in part, because parents are afraid of being perceived by other village members as challenging social norms – in a context where more than four out of ten girls marry before reaching legal age.

Read more:

HAENNI, Simon, and Guilherme LICHAND (2021) "Harming to Signal: Child Marriage Vs. Public Donations in Malawi", Available at SSRN: https://ssrn.com/abstract=3633803.

The cases highlighted above illustrate the opportunities and challenges of leveraging social expectations and social image concerns to change behaviors with public consequences around the world. In some contexts, it is not hard to come up with ways to decrease the visibility of certain actions in order to mitigate negative behaviors motivated by social pressure (as in the case of the "honor roll"), or to increase the visibility of other actions to amplify positive behaviors (as in the case of vaccination).

In other settings, such as those of child marriage or low female labor force participation, trying to incorporate these mechanisms into policy design seems more complex at first. Luckily, as we will see in the following chapters, there are cost-effective and relatively simple ways to correct inaccurate social expectations (as in the case of female labor market participation in Saudi Arabia) or to dismantle negative social norms (as in the case of child marriage in Malawi), by taking behavioral insights to heart when designing policies to address these mechanisms.

4.3 Self-Control Problems

Next, we will discuss the sources of real citizens'self-control problems and the implications of the inconsistencies they generate between their plans and actual actions.

4.3.1 Impulsivity

The easiest way to think about self-control issues is as if they were a problem of "multiple selves," whereby the "controlled self" strictly follows plans, while the "uncontrolled self" always acts on impulses. Depending on which "self" prevails in a particular decision, that decision may or may not be consistent with the original plans. We have all made impulsive decisions at some point. The best symptom of this is regret – back in the "controlled" state, our present "self" wishes that she had made the decision rather than the other "self" (see Fig. 4.4).

As we saw in our examples of drinking and driving, in the presence of negative externalities, impulsive private decisions can have dramatic public consequences. The same logic applies to impulsive consumption, chronic indebtedness, or acts of violence – all with high private and public costs.

Restraining impulsivity through policy is a huge challenge. Recent evidence shows that cognitive-behavioral therapy can be effective in developing self-control and preventing violence, crime, and incarceration among disadvantaged populations.

4.3.2 Procrastination

In the case of procrastination (or, more generally, of intertemporal inconsistencies[3]), the conflict between "selfs" manifests itself by contraposing the "present self" to the "future selfs." Many studies show that a significant fraction of the

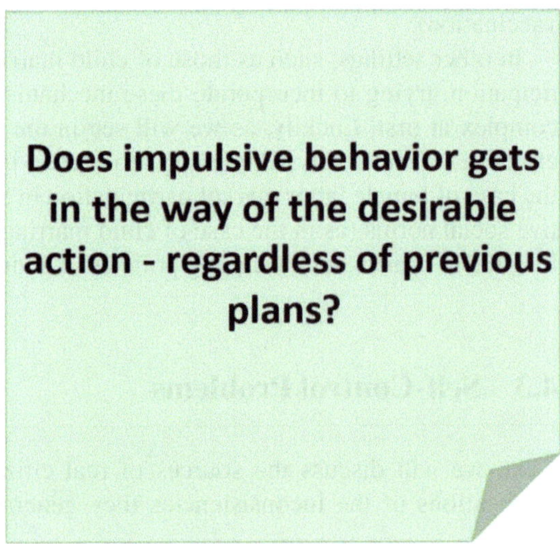

Fig. 4.4 Impulsivity. (Source: Provided by the Authors)

[3] In economics, we call temporal inconsistencies when the intertemporal dimension of public policies is taken into account, so that a decision that seems optimal in the short run may not be so in the long run. According to its creators (Finn E. Kydland and Edward C. Prescott), intertemporal inconsistency would happen because individuals' expectations about the policies to be followed in the future by the government have a great impact on the present behavior of policies, so that if citizens are sure that the government will maintain a certain policy, which is well accepted, then the government can "afford" to deviate from this policy in the short run, because individuals will continue to believe that the policy holds in the long run. Analogously, applied to the behavioral

population – especially among the poor – tends to be too optimistic about their willingness to bear costs in the future. In concrete terms, this means that my "present self" does not want to go to the gym or study now, but thinks it will be willing to do so in the future. It turns out that when the future finally becomes present, the procrastination cycle repeats itself (see Fig. 4.5).

One way to explain why people procrastinate is to appeal to this excessive optimism about the future (which economists call *present bias*[4,5]). Interestingly, even those who can anticipate abandoning their plans in the future have difficulty in ensuring that their actions are consistent with past plans.

It is difficult to mitigate the consequences of intertemporal inconsistencies through interventions. Solutions are usually costly and, to take them up, individuals have to bear costs in the present, while benefiting only in the future. An example is a piggy bank that only allows one to collect the coins accumulated in it once it is full. Another is a bank account that does not allow you to withdraw before a certain deadline without a penalty.

There are intertemporal inconsistencies of various kinds, each of which requiring different commitment devices to ensure actions consistent with previous plans. A recent study in Malawi showed that a significant proportion of mothers make ambitious plans to allocate more resources to their children in the future, but change

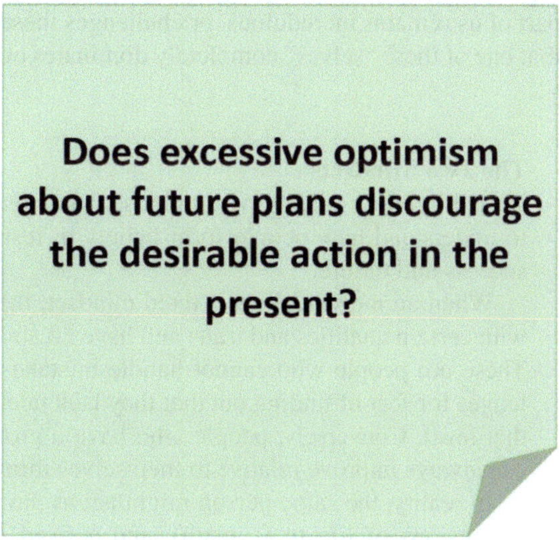

Fig. 4.5 Procrastination. (Source: Provided by the Authors)

sciences, this is when they will have certain behaviors in the long run, but this is not when the "future" arrives.

[4] Present bias is a leading explanation for important public problems such as low savings. Your "present self" might not be so willing to save today, deferring the costs of foregoing consumption to the "future self" – who she thinks will willfully bear these costs.

[5] Economists split present-biased subjects into "sophisticated" ones, those who anticipate that they will not follow through on past plans even in the future, and "naive" ones, who do not anticipate their intertemporal inconsistencies.

their minds as that future approaches (even when it has not yet arrived!). An example would be plans (eventually foregone) to save more in the future to pay for their college tuition down the line. Some parents might start allocating a small fraction of their savings to finance these expenses, with ambitious plans to increase that fraction in the future, but, as time goes by, ultimately reallocate these resources to other needs, subtracting from the savings earmarked to their children before (or to a greater extent) relative to other savings.

This kind of inconsistency (called *parent bias*) is not about reallocating planned resources from the future to the present, but rather, about reallocating planned resources from children to their parents (as the time frame to the actual use of these resources becomes closer). Children often have no bearing over the plans or decisions ultimately made by their parents. As such, they are extremely vulnerable to such intertemporal preference reversals.

4.3.3 Limiting Mental Models

Limiting mental models refer to self-image conflicts. We have all experienced such conflicts between different perceptions of ourselves: part of us believes that we are capable of changing something, or that the effort will be worthwhile, while another part of us remains incredulous, or challenges these beliefs. Ultimately, it is possible that one of these "selves" completely dominates our plans and actions (see Fig. 4.6).

The Two Mindsets

"Fixed mindset" and "growth mindset" are concepts developed in an attempt to understand how people form beliefs in responses to their experiences of success and failure.

When an individual has a fixed mindset, they believe that they were born with certain qualities and traits and have no ability to change or obtain others. These are people who cannot handle mistakes and who tend to avoid challenges for fear of finding out that they lack talent or intelligence to succeed at that level. Conversely, people who have a growth mindset believe that they can always improve relative to themselves through effort.

In reality, the same person might act as having a growth mindset in some dimensions of life (e.g., math), and a fixed mindset in others (e.g., arts). Strikingly, external circumstances can quickly change how individuals express these beliefs even within the same dimension. Because some of these circumstances, such as cognitive load, also tend to affect impulsivity and procrastination, this is what leads us to categorize limiting mental models as part of self-control problems.

Read more:

DWECK, C. S. (2006). Mindset: the new psychology of success. New York, Random House.

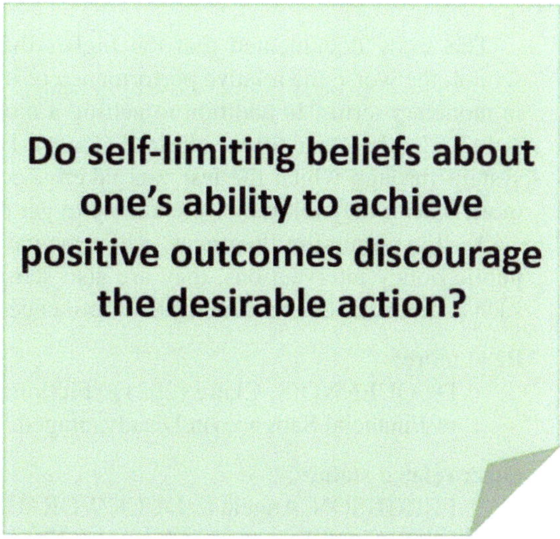

Fig. 4.6 Limiting mental models. (Source: Provided by the Authors)

If mental models reflect beliefs (e.g., about the sources of success), why do we classify this mechanism as a self-control problem? Scientific studies document that external factors systematically affect how these mental models manifest. Specifically, when other demands compete for subjects' mental bandwidth (e.g., when we try to record a phone number in our memory instead of writing it down on our cell phone), it becomes more difficult to exercise self-control, increasing the prevalence of impulsive behaviors and procrastination. Similarly, under cognitive load, limiting mental models become more dominant.

When students are told that their teacher does not believe that someone who does not know math can ever be good at it, they immediately behave as if they have fixed mindsets – even those who, just before, had expressed beliefs that intelligence is not something fixed that cannot be changed. This is indicative that different mental models coexist within each of us (as if they were different "selfs"!).

Ultimately, which mental model eventually "wins" may depend on the external environment and the extent to which it imposes cognitive load. Along those lines, students from disadvantaged backgrounds tend to have a higher prevalence of fixed mindset. Similarly, financial concerns (such as "will my salary last until the end of the month?" or "will I have enough money to buy food for my children?") also tend to make adults display limiting mental models to a greater extent.

Financial Worries and Student Math Performance in the United States
A study in the United States assessed student performance in simple math questions (such as computing a percentage or computing the mean of a string of numbers), distinguishing when the questions were framed in monetary terms or in some nonmonetary unit (e.g., cookies or the number of emails filtered through the spam box).

The study documented that the higher the share of poor students in a school, the worse the relative performance of its students in questions framed in monetary terms. In addition to getting a much lower number of questions right under these conditions, these students asked for more hints in the online system through which the test was taken – consistent with limiting mental models, as if they felt they were unable to get them right without help.

As this discussion illustrates, while mental models may be malleable by public policy interventions, they are also sensitive to other external factors, such as financial concerns and social influences.

Read more:

DUQUENNOIS, Claire (2021) "Fictional Money, Real Costs: Impacts of Financial Salience on Disadvantaged Students", mimeo.

Other related studies:

FERGUSON, Angela L. DUCKWORTH, and Carol S. DWECK (2019) "A National Experiment Reveals Where a Growth Mindset Improves Achievement," Nature, 573, pp. 364–369.

JOB, Veronika, Carol S. DWECK, and Gregory WALTON (2010) "Ego Depletion – Is It All In Your Head? Implicit Theories About Willpower Affect Self-Regulation," Psychological Science, 21(11), pp. 1686–93.

As we will see later, some mental models can be manipulated by relatively simple interventions. Studies show that it is possible to make students come to believe that, with effort, they can always improve relative to themselves. The study documents that the idea that the brain, just like a muscle, "gets stronger when it exercises," has the potential to convert fixed mindsets into growth mindsets.

4.4 Inattention Problems

Next, we will discuss the sources of real citizens'inattention problems and their implications – as they often prevent financial costs and benefits from being perfectly evaluated in the decision-making process.

4.4.1 *Cognitive Biases*

Did you know that a typical brain runs on less energy than the light bulb in your fridge? The only way to navigate a complex world with so little energy is to process information extremely efficiently, distributing limited mental bandwidth between attention, memory, and impulse control. This efficient processing, however, comes at the expense of shortcuts in decision-making – it is necessary to cut corners, following rules of thumb that allow us to survive successfully even without having to process every stimulus at every decision. While most of the time these shortcuts lead to the right choice (the result of our adaptive abilities selected over thousands of years), in some cases, they can induce systematic errors – the so-called cognitive biases.

There is a vast literature documenting systematic biases that influence how individuals make decisions. These biases are so named because they are considered "anomalies": they should not affect the decisions of the "ideal citizen." For instance, when individuals are given the opportunity to choose from a number of options displayed on a form with one of them already pre-marked – the default option – there is a tendency to stick with that default. Experiments verify this by showing that the distribution of alternatives chosen changes systematically with which of the options is set as the default (even when this is determined by lottery!). This phenomenon is called *status quo bias*.

The most known manifestation of this phenomenon is the organ donation form, which we discussed in the previous chapter. Different countries use different default options: in countries like Denmark, the Netherlands, and Germany, the default option is "NO", while in countries like Austria, Poland, and Hungary, the default option is "YES." In line with default bias, only 4.25% of the population are organ donors in Denmark, 27.5% in the Netherlands, and 12% in Germany; in contrast to 99.9% in Austria and Hungary, and 99.5% in Poland. One might wonder if there are other cultural factors impacting this, but some of the countries in different groups are too similar for other factors to explain away such striking differences in the proportion of donors. Moreover, an experimental study documents that the default option in fact induces systematic differences in the decision to become an organ donor.

Another well-known cognitive bias is the *decoy effect*. When the "ideal citizen" considers an alternative as superior to another in a binary choice, introducing an unattractive third option – which is never chosen in binary choices against any of the two other alternatives – should not affect the outcome of the former choice. It turns out that this odd option (the "decoy"), when craftily presented, might end up making the option that would not be chosen at first more attractive in comparison. This is because the real citizen uses decision heuristics; in particular, processing information by contrasting options rather than by merely considering each alternative on its own.

This happens more often than you might think. Who has never noticed that airlines often offer odd routes – for instance with more stops, but with a higher price tag? Are there people who buy such peculiar routes? If not, why do airlines do this? It is because, in the presence of these odd routes, other routes that would typically be considered expensive are likely perceived as cheaper and advantageous in comparison.

There are many other cognitive biases, all of which derive from the brain's need to make decisions under limited mental bandwidth. What they all have in common

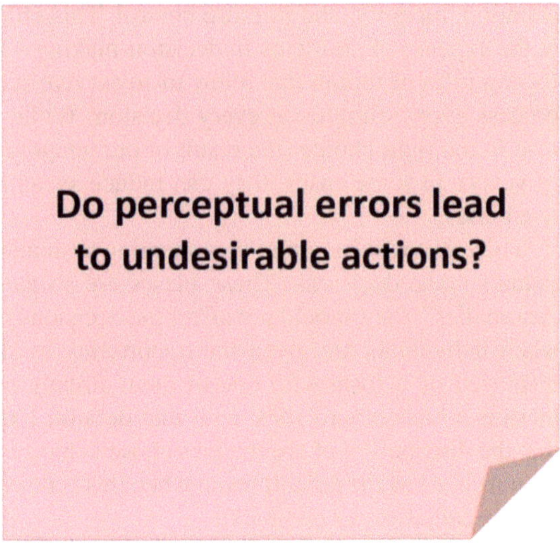

Fig. 4.7 Cognitive biases. (Source: Provided by the Authors)

is that, in the face of limited capacity to process all stimuli, elements of the so-called choice architecture capture individuals' attention, distorting their choices relative to the ideal citizen (who has unlimited capacity to process information) (see Fig. 4.7).

As the discussion above illustrates, attention could be reallocated by public policy tools that affect how different options are displayed (including default options). Attention can also be reallocated by other external factors, such as financial concerns – which we discuss below.

4.4.2 *Cognitive Load*

A number of studies reveal that scarcity of different kinds (of attention, of energy, of money, and even of social interactions) competes for our limited cognitive resources. The more tired we are (or thirsty or hungry), the less attention we are able to devote to reading a chapter in this book, and the less self-control we are able to mobilize to resist a chocolate bar. Cognitive psychologists call this phenomenon cognitive load (see Fig. 4.8).

Recent research documents that poverty – a permanent state of financial scarcity – and its accompanying financial worries also capture attention, memory, and impulse control. In previous sections, we have discussed how the expression of different mental models can be affected by the cognitive load associated with financial worries. The same is also true when it comes to inattention.

Cognitive load means that the decisions of poorer individuals are more vulnerable to cognitive biases and, thus, to costly mistakes. At the same time, the poorest have the least room in their budget to accommodate the consequences of such mistakes.

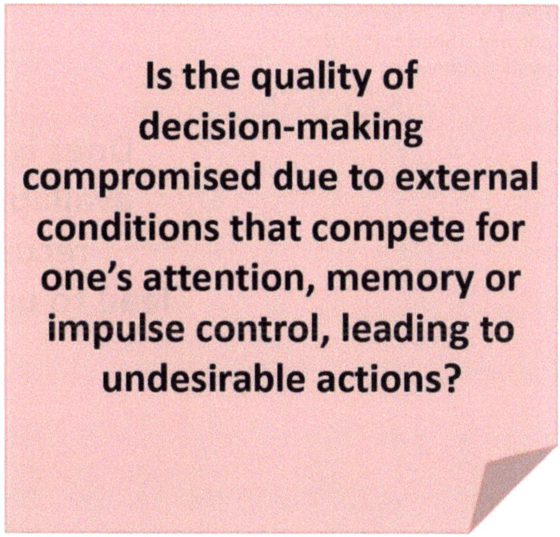

Fig. 4.8 Cognitive load. (Source: Provided by the Authors)

Mitigating the effects of cognitive load is not easy. Nonetheless, acknowledging it can be key to modify the choice architecture, especially for the poor – often the main target audience for public service delivery.

4.4.3 Learning Through Noticing

Cognitive biases are often discussed in contexts where the decision is made only once (as in the example of organ donation) or infrequently (as in the case of purchasing an airline ticket). Do these biases also apply to decisions that need to be made every day? (see Fig. 4.9).

A few studies illustrate that the answer to this question is affirmative. Seaweed farmers in Indonesia ignore the fact that some neighboring farmers are systematically more productive because they use slightly different settings for their equipment – even though they handle this equipment every day. Analogously, in Brazil, parents of public school students tend not to follow their children's school life closely; in particular, they tend to underestimate the number of classes they miss – even though schools send report cards home with truancy information every quarter.

These systematic failures to update beliefs (and change behavior accordingly) even when information is available at low or no cost is what we call *learning through noticing*. In the examples above, farmers who use better settings and parents who are better informed experience, in each case, better outcomes in the present (e.g., higher profits, for the former) and better expected outcomes in the future (e.g., better employment and wage prospects, for the latter).

Interventions that attempt to reallocate attention to the relevant attributes of the decision at hand tend to help individuals to learn through noticing. Drawing

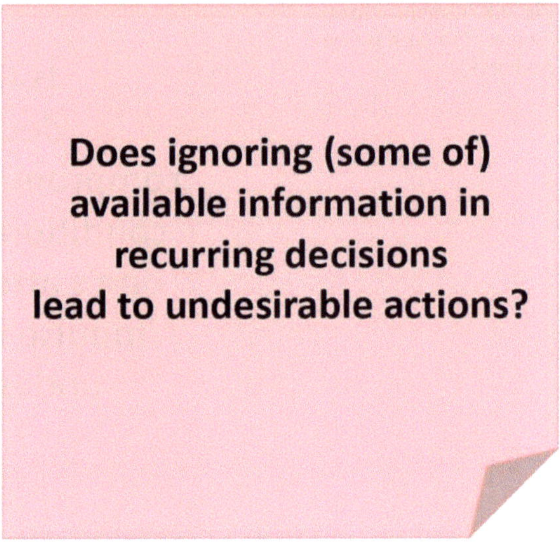

Fig. 4.9 Learning through noticing. (Source: Provided by the Authors)

Table 4.1 MSI framework overview

Motivation	Self-control	Inattention
Intrinsic motivation	Impulsivity	Cognitive biases
Social pressure	Procrastination	Cognitive load
Social image concerns	Limiting mental models	Learning through noticing

Source: Provided by the Authors

farmers' attention to the settings chosen to operate their equipment – even without telling them about which setting is best for their particular circumstances, which might be hard to assess – and reallocating parents' attention to their children's school life – even without informing them about their children's attendance, which might be hard to track at high frequency – might induce them to collect the decision-relevant information themselves. If they do so, their decisions will tend to converge to those of the ideal citizen.

4.5 Limitations

As we anticipated, the MSI framework (see Table 4.1) leaves out some behavioral mechanisms that are widely studied in behavioral economics, cognitive psychology, or social psychology. Below, we will briefly discuss the reasons for this methodological choice and point out some policy-relevant phenomena that require a broader outlook than that offered by our methodology.

The two main inclusion criteria for the MSI framework were that the mechanisms chosen should be (1) simple to understand, and (2) relevant to almost any policy area – not just to some specific sectors. In this sense, motivation, self-control, and inattention problems are relatively intuitive and extremely prevalent, present in basically every area of government-citizen interaction. As we shall see, this is not necessarily true for other behavioral phenomena, even if they might be extremely relevant for some specific sectors.

In particular, the MSI framework does not encompass risk preferences. Different individuals can be more averse or prone to risk. People who are more risk-averse tend to prefer alternatives with safer returns (such as those who prefer a tenured public sector position over a private sector job, even if they expect to earn more in the private sector). Others prefer to bet on an uncertain income, expressing greater tolerance for risk. Some people tend to care about losses much more than about equivalent gains (a phenomenon known as *loss aversion*). Loss aversion is a behavioral mechanism, because the "ideal citizen" should not treat equivalent gains and losses differently (especially when they are small relative to their wealth). The "real citizen," on the other hand, tends to be risk-averse in the domain of gains, but a "risk lover" in the domain of losses. This mechanism has implications for the demand for insurance, for instance.

Another behavioral mechanism that has implications for insurance demand and that is not part of the MSI framework is *ambiguity aversion*. The real citizen that is ambiguity-averse makes decisions under risk considering only the "worst-case scenario" – overlooking information about the other scenarios (something that the ideal citizen would never do!). As a result of ambiguity aversion, demand for index insurance (which protects individuals from losses only when such losses are widespread) tends to be very low. The reason is that ambiguity aversion leads "real farmers" to only think about the worst case in which they pay for insurance, lose their harvest, and still do not get paid – because aggregate losses in his or her region were not large enough to warrant payout (what is known as "basis risk").

Public policies related to insurance provision or risk management need to go beyond the MSI framework. These mechanisms, however, are not easily understood by professionals without a background in economics or actuarial science, nor are they obviously relevant to other government sectors.

The MSI framework also does not encompass social preferences. The "real citizen" is not exclusively concerned with his or her own well-being, nor does he or she ignore collective or social goals. Some individuals make decisions accounting for some sense of justice (e.g., displaying *inequality aversion*[6]) and displaying *reciprocity.*[7] In particular, a significant share of individuals is willing to give up financial resources so that other people could access more resources. While this could be framed as an element of intrinsic motivation – thus covered by the MSI framework –,

---

[6] Inequality aversion represents preferences that value an equitable distribution of resources. Inequity-averse subjects are willing to punish others who deviate from that behavior, even at a cost.

[7] Reciprocity represents preferences that value treating others the same way they feel they are treated by them. Negative reciprocity entails that subjects may respond to offers considered unfair in a harsh and even cruel way, while negative reciprocity entails that, when they feel well-treated, people respond with fair offers.

it has broader implications, for example, for how citizens vote or what policies they are willing to support.

The MSI framework bypasses these discussions because we focus on the technical aspects of policy design to correct externalities, ignoring the political complexities of mobilizing resources to implement them, or garnering support to approve them. Evidently, social preferences are extremely relevant as part of the political context in which policymaking occurs. As such, recognizing them should be part of the repertoire of all public agents interested in working within the institutional constraints of policy design and implementation.

Summary

1. This chapter introduced a novel framework for diagnosing policy-relevant behavioral mechanisms: the MSI framework.
2. The framework departs from the realization that individuals do not respond exclusively to financial incentives. Rather, their behaviors are conditioned by cognitive, emotional, and social constraints.
3. The chapter discussed how real citizens' motivation problems – those linked to intrinsic motivation, social expectations, and social image concerns –; self-control problems – impulsivity, procrastination, and limiting mental models –; and inattention problems – those linked to cognitive biases, cognitive load, and learning through noticing – can influence how individuals make plans and behave, and how private decisions mediated by these behavioral mechanisms can have critical public consequences – from externalities to social inequalities.

Suggested Readings

JOHNSON, Eric, and Daniel GOLDSTEIN (2003) "Do Defaults Save Lives?", **Science,** v. 302(5649), pp. 1338–1339, november. 2003.

LICHAND, Guilherme, BETTINGER, Eric, CUNHA, Nina, and MADEIRA, Ricardo (2020) "The Psychological Effects of Poverty on Investments in Children's Human Capital", **SSRN**, p. 77, january. 2022. Available at SSRN: https://ssrn.com/abstract=3644127.

MANI, Anandi, MULLAINATHAN, Sendhil, SHAFIR, Eldar, and Jiaying ZHAO (2013) "Poverty Impedes Cognitive Function", **Science**, v. 341(6149), pp. 976–980, august. 2013.

SHAFIR, Eldar and MULLAINATHAN, Sendhil (2013) "Scarcity: Why Having Too Little Means So Much", **Times Books**, september. 2013.

SHAH, Anuj K, MULLAINATHAN, Sendhil, and SHAFIR, Eldar (2012a) "Some Consequences of Having Too Little", **Science**, 338 (6107), pp. 682–685, november. 2012.

SHAH, Anuj K, SHAFIR, Eldar, and MULLAINATHAN, Sendhil (2015) "Scarcity Frames Value", **Psychological Science**, 26 (4), pp. 402–412, february. 2015.

WOODFORD, Michael (2020) "Modeling Imprecision in Perception, Valuation, and Choice", **Annual Review of Economics**, 12, pp. 579–601, august. 2020.

BURSZTYN, Leonardo, FUJIWARA, Thomas, and PALLAIS, Amanda (2017) "'Acting Wife': Marriage Market Incentives and Labor Market Investments", **The American Economic Review** 107, 11, pp. 3288–3319, november. 2017.

BURSZTYN, Leonardo, GONZALES, Alessandra, and YANAGIZAWA-DROTT, David (2020) "Misperceived Social Norms: Female Labor Force Participation in Saudi Arabia", **The American Economic Review**, 110 (10), pp. 2997–3029.

CURRARINI, Sergio, and MENGEL, Friederike (2016) “Identity, Homophily and In-group Bias”, **European Economic Review**, 90, pp. 40–55

FRACCHIA, Mattia, MOLINA, Teresa, and VICENTE, Pedro (2019) “Incentivizing Community Health Workers in Guine-Bissau: Experimental Evidence on Social Status and Intrinsic Motivation”, Sierra Leone, december. 2018 (mimeo).

FRYER, Roland, and TORELLI, Paul (2010) “An Empirical Analysis of ‘Acting White’”, **Journal of Public Economics**, 94 (5–6), pp. 380–396.

HAENNI, Simon, and LICHAND, Guilherme (2021) “Harming to Signal: Child Marriage Vs. Public Donations in Malawi”, **SSRN**, março. 2021. Available at SSRN: https://ssrn.com/abstract=3633803.

KARING, Anne (2021) “Social Signaling and Childhood Immunization: A Field Experiment in Sierra Leone”. 2021 (mimeo)

LICHAND, Guilherme, and WOLF, Sharon (2021) “Arm-Wrestling in the Classroom: The Non-Monotonic Effects of Monitoring Teachers”, **SSRN**. 2021. Available at SSRN: https://ssrn.com/abstract=3662146.

CASABURI, Lorenzo, and Willis, Jack (2018) “Time Vs. State Insurance: Experimental Evidence From Contract Farming in Kenya”, **The American Economic Review**, vol. 108(2), pp. 3778–3813

CLARO, Susana, PAUNESKU, David, and DWECK, Carol S. (2016) “Growth Mindset Tempers the Effects of Poverty on Academic Achievement”, **PNAS**, 113(31), pp. 8664–8668

DIZON-ROSS, Rebecca, and ZUCKER, Ariel (2021) “Can Price Discrimination Incentivize Behavior Change? Evidence From a Randomized Field Experiment”, maio. 2021 (mimeo).

COHEN, Jessica, and PASCALINE, Dupas (2010) “Free Distribution or Cost-Sharing? Evidence from a Randomized Malaria Prevention Experiment, **The Quarterly Journal of Economics**, vol. 125, Issue 1, pp. 1–45 https://doi.org/10.1162/qjec.2010.125.1.1

DUFLO, Esther, KREMER, Michael, and ROBINSON, Jonathan (2011) “Nudging Farmers to Use Fertilizer: Theory and Experimental Evidence from Kenya”, **The American Economic Review**, vol. 101(6), pp. 2350–90

DUQUENNOIS, Claire (2021) “Fictional Money, Real Costs: Impacts of Financial Salience on Disadvantaged Students”, mimeo.

HAUSHOFER, Johannes, and FEHR, Ernst (2014) “On The Psychology of Poverty”, **Science**, vol. 344(6186), pp. 862–867

HELLER, Sara, POLLACK, Harold, ANDER, Roseanna, and LUDWIG, Jens (2013) “Preventing Youth Violence and Dropout: A Randomized Field Experiment”, **National Bureau of Economic Research**, 19014, may. 2013.

JOB, Veronika, DWECK, Carol S, and WALTON, Gregory (2010) “Ego Depletion – Is It All In Your Head? Implicit Theories About Willpower Affect Self-Regulation”, **Psychological Science**, vol. 21(11), pp. 1686–93. 2010.

LICHAND, Guilherme, and THIBAUD, Juliette (2020) “Parent-Bias”, **SSRN**. Available at SSRN: https://ssrn.com/abstract=3737685.

SCHILBACH, Frank (2019) “Alcohol and Self-Control: A Field Experiment in India”, **The American Economic Review**, vol. 109(4), pp. 1290–1322

SHAH, Anuj K, MULLAINATHAN, Sendhil, and SHAFIR, Eldar (2012b) “Some Consequences of Having Too Little”, **Science**, vol. 338(6107), pp. 682–685

SHIV, Baba, and FEDORIKHIN, Alexander (1999) “Heart and Mind in Conflict: The Interplay of Affect and Cognition in Consumer Decision Making”, **Journal of Consumer Research**, vol. 26(3), pp. 278–292

YEAGER, David S. et al. (2019) “A National Experiment Reveals Where a Growth Mindset Improves Achievement”, **Nature**, vol. 573, pp. 364–369

FEHR, EMST E SCHMIDT, Klaus M (1999) “A Theory of Fairness, Competition, and Cooperation, Artigo, **The Quarterly Journal of Economics**, vol. 114 (3), pp. 817–868

GNEEZY, Uri and RUSTICHINI, Aldo “A Fine is a Price”, **Journal of Legal Studies**, vol. 29, n. 1, January. 2000. Available at SSRN: https://ssrn.com/abstract=180117

Philip J. Cook and Ludwig, Jens. "Weighing the "Burden of 'Acting White'": Are There Race Differences in Attitudes toward Education?", **Journal of Policy Analysis and Management**, pp. 256–78, vol. 16, 2. 1997.

Dweck, Carol S. (2017) "**Mindset** : a nova psicologia do sucesso". Tradução de S. Duarte. 1a ed. São Paulo: Objetiva, 312 p, janeiro. 2017.

Abadie, A. & Gay, S. (2006). The impact of presumed consent legislation on cadaveric organ donation: a cross country study. **Journal of Health Economics**, vol. 25, pp. 599–620

Alliance, O (2007). Final report: Alliance-O, European group for coordination of national research programmes on organ donation and transplantation 2004–2007. 2007.

Council of Europe (2012). Transplant Newsletter. International Figures on Organ Donation and Transplantation Activity. Year 2011, Strasbourg: Council of Europe. 2012.

Bouwman, R., Lie, J., Bomhoff, M., Friele, R.D. Study on the set-up of organ donation and transplantation in the EU Member States, uptake and impact of the EU Action Plan on Organ Donation and Transplantation (2009–2015). 2013.

Lichand, Guilherme and Christen, Julien and van Egeraat, Eppie (2022) "Do Behavioral Nudges Work Under Remote Learning? Evidence from Brazil During the Pandemic", **SSRN**, University of Zurich, Department of Economics, n. 363, april. 2022. Available at SSRN: https://ssrn.com/abstract=3724386 or https://doi.org/10.2139/ssrn.3724386

Thaler, Richard & Benartzi, Shlomo. (2007). Heuristics and Biases in Retirement Savings Behavior. **Journal of Economic Perspectives**. vol. 21. n. 3, pp. 81–104, August. 2007. Available at: https://doi.org/10.1257/jep.21.3.81.

Chapter 5
Motivating the Use of Systems Thinking

5.1 Introduction

A system can be defined as an interconnected set of elements that is organized in order to achieve some goal. From a systems theory point of view, everything that is known is part of a system and is usually embedded in larger systems. A common example is in biology: organs are made up of tissues, which can be defined as systems of interdependent cells that perform a given function together. Cells, in turn, are made up of organelles, a set of intracellular elements that are also interdependent in performing their functions. Zooming out, organs are part of systems, such as the digestive and nervous systems, which together maintain a larger living system, the body.

There are several ways to delimit systems. For example, one can define delimitations of geography, production and market, culture, or even related to government policies (e.g., health, education, public safety). However, when it comes to social or public policy systems, system delimitations cannot be artificial. A public policy system is always purpose-driven: State interventions are ultimately seeking to generate a preestablished outcome, so these systems were created and delimited to achieve a goal and purpose.

Thus, in this book, when we discuss the concept of a system, we refer to a set of stakeholders, regulations, physical structures, services, technologies, and organizations that, through interactions among themselves, seek to achieve a result based on a purpose. This perspective allows for a different perception than that of linear models, in which an input in a unidirectional cause-and-effect chain generates desired outcomes. In the systemic model, the relationships between the different

[1] Archetypes are models that explain common systems dynamics. These models are tools for systems thinking practitioners to analyze and categorize systems maps.

G. Lichand et al., *Behavioral Insights for Policy Design*,
https://doi.org/10.1007/978-3-031-33034-6_5

Table 5.1 Linear model to systemic model

Linear model	Systemic model
Unidirectional causality	Multidirectional causality
Effects in linear chains	Effects in circular chains
Elements receive input and generate output	Elements receive input and generate output, which may return as input in a feedback loop
Proportionality between input and output	Inputs can generate disproportionate outputs

Source: Provided by the Authors

Table 5.2 Cynefin model

Complex
Flow and unpredictability
No right answers, only emergent interventions
Probe, sense, respond
Complicated
Expert diagnosis required
Cause-effect relationships are discoverable, but not immediately obvious. There is more than one possible answer
Sense, analyze, respond
Chaotic
High turbulence
No clear cause-effect relationships
Act, sense, respond
Ordered
Repetitive patterns and consistent events
Cause-effect relationships are clear and correct answers exist
Sense, categorize, respond

Source: Provided by the Authors

components of the system model a nonlinear cause-and-effect dynamic. As such, the systemic model can incorporate the complexity of the real world, something the linear and ordered models fail to do (see Table 5.1).

5.1.1 *Complexity*

When we observe public policy systems, it is common to note that there is a large number of and diversity amongst stakeholders, structures, regulations, and technologies, as well as diverse relationships amongst the various parts of these systems. We refer to this scenario as complex, that is, the cause-and-effect relationships in this system are not immediately clear, generating ambiguity and uncertainty about how the system works.

In general, we can differentiate four different contexts: orderly, complicated, complex, and chaotic (see Table 5.2). These domains explain a gradation in the level of complexity in situations, ranging from what can be easily known to the level of apparent absence of cause-and-effect relationships.

The four domains represent different situations for decision-making and action. It is common to seek to operate in the complicated and ordered domains, where there are clear answers to known or knowable questions. But in public policy systems, we often find ourselves in complex or even chaotic systems when there is a crisis. Therefore, it is important to recognize the aspects of complexity in order to navigate public policy systems.

Complexity is a phenomenon that results from interactions of the elements that make up our world, in multiple ways, without an apparent greater order. Like systems, complexity is part of the human experience, since we are immersed in complex systems. This concept, applied to systems logic, aims to explain the relationships between the parts of a system and the effects or behaviors it generates.

5.1.2 Complex Systems

Complex systems are characterized by specific properties, resulting from the interaction between their parts and with their surroundings. For example, social systems arise from the interaction between the individuals that compose them, just as a thought is generated by the relationship between neurons in the brain. It is important to know what features characterize complex systems, which can be described as general rules.

5.1.2.1 Emergence

Complex systems have aggregate behaviors. For example, fire ants build huge colonies, which are capable of complex behaviors as a system, such as going to war against other colonies, using its individuals to create bridges with their own bodies to overcome collective obstacles, and dividing up work by "castes." Emergence is the name given to the relationship between the behaviors that can be observed at the system level and the properties of the elements (nodes) of the system. In this example, emergence is in the various factors in the biology of the ants that allow them to relate to each other in complex ways to produce the aggregate behaviors of the colony.

5.1.2.2 Nonlinearity

Linearity is an important aspect of noncomplex systems: the relationship between additional inputs and outputs is constant. In complex systems, in turn, the rate at which additional inputs translate into outputs is not linear; it might depend, among other parameters, on the system's initial state. For example, a person who leaves his cool air-conditioned office and goes for a walk on a hot sidewalk does not experience a change in body temperature in the same proportion as his surroundings since his body has complex mechanisms to control its internal temperature. Nonlinearity can play in the opposite way, with a small input triggering a large output, such as a spark causing a forest fire.

5.1.2.3 Interdependence

Interdependence refers to the integration between parts of a system, even though they appear to be loosely related. For example, the balance of an ecosystem depends on the species that compose it. If one species is removed from an ecosystem, or an exotic one is introduced, this affects all the other components in the ecosystem. This phenomenon is explained by the interdependence of the parts of the system. The ability of the system to resist changes such as these is called resilience.

5.1.2.4 Openness

Complex systems are never entirely closed – there are always exchanges between a system and its environment. Thus, systems vary in the openness of their boundaries, with clearer delimitations such as that of living organisms, or softer delimitations such as the transition belt between two biomes. In public policy systems, the delimitations are even more blurred. For example, an educational system can be delimited into a school or a school community, taking into account the family of the students. Both delimitations have different consequences for analyses and understandings of that system. Therefore, an analysis of a public policy system is influenced by the intentions of those who analyze it – a good system map is not an exhaustive system, but a system that produces concrete answers to relevant questions.

5.1.2.5 Nodes

Nodes are the individual components that relate to each other to make up the system. Like the parts of a car, a single node or a set of nodes does not explain the whole system, it is necessary to observe them all together and understand their connections. The nodes can be stakeholders, events, factors, values, structures, among several other possibilities. In this book, we will treat nodes as variables, that is, quantitative or qualitative values that can increase or decrease. Examples of quantitative nodes include: amount of liters of water, Internet speed, amount of money in the current account. Examples of qualitative variables, on the other hand, include: level of fear, perception of effort, and feeling of tiredness.

5.1.2.6 Connections

Connections are the relationships between the nodes of a system. These connections represent the nonlinear aspect of the system: a node can connect to one or more other nodes, which in turn connect to other elements of the system, forming a network of complex relationships. Often these relationships create cycles – virtuous, vicious, or of equilibrium. Mapping connections is fundamental to understand a complex system. Various systemic behaviors can only be analyzed by describing the quality of connections.

5.1.2.7 Function

A fundamental aspect of public policy systems is the function of the system. A function is a desired goal or state of operation of the system, its intention or purpose. For example, the function of schools is student learning. It is important to take into consideration that, despite being a desired goal, the system does not always operate in a functional way. Often, the results of the system differ from its function, such as a school that fails to generate learning. Comprehending the function of a system is central to understanding the relationships between its elements and the results it produces.

Limits of Success: An Example of a System

Limits to Success is a system archetype,[1] that is, a very common story that repeats itself in many contexts. The "limits to success" system archetype occurs when a cycle of effort and result encounters a third factor that limits the effectiveness of the effort.

Dieting is a good example: usually, losing the first 5 kilos is much easier than losing the last 2 kilos. When we diet, we decrease our calorie intake, which makes us lose weight and encourages us to maintain the dieting behavior. However, over time, the body adjusts its metabolism to a lower amount of calories, thus limiting the effect of dieting on the result in weight loss. The diagram in Fig. 5.1 illustrates this dynamic.

What Is Happening?

There is an effort that generates a result, and the result stimulates more effort. At some point, the result reaches a plateau – the effectiveness of the effort is limited by another factor. The more effort is increased to overcome this limit, the more the system responds back, further limiting the results.

If we could see the evolution of this system in a graph, we would have the picture in Fig. 5.2.

This example shows how the relationships in a system are complex and go in many directions, generating cycles. We will discuss this further in the following sections of this book.

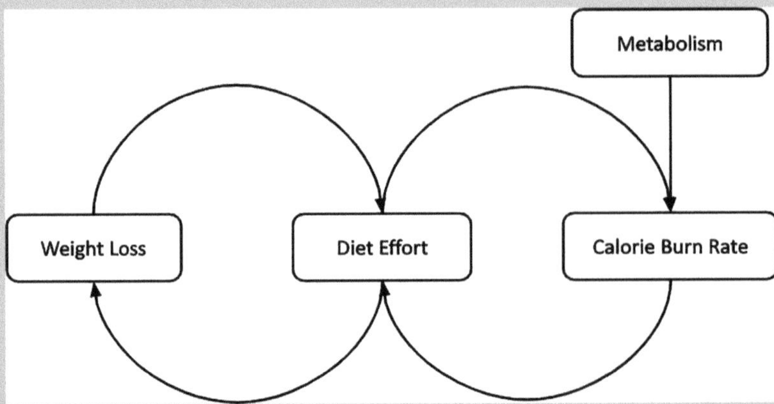

Fig. 5.1 The system of weight loss. (Source: Provided by the Author)

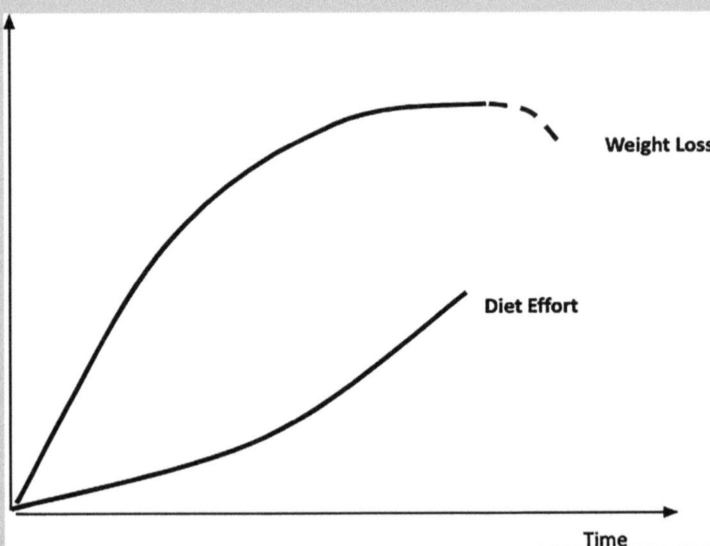

Fig. 5.2 The system's chart. (Source: Provided by the Author)

5.2 Why Systems Thinking Matters for Policy Design

Over the past decades, governments have been concerned with managing complicated issues with linear relationships that are ultimately predictable, such as banking regulations, taxes, and infrastructure projects. But the public sector faces, and must deal with, complex problems, that is, those marked by a high degree of uncertainty. Complex problems arise when there is little predictability, mostly because cause-and-effect relationships are not linear and often are understood only in retrospect. Many of these complex problems are also known as wicked problems, characterized by a high degree of ambiguity and uncertainty, with no defined beginning or end, that are interconnected, multicausal, and cannot be solved completely.

If we start from the idea that society is organized in social systems, we can say that wicked problems are unwanted outcomes of that system. In other words, a social system that produces dysfunctional results creates social problems which can only be solved by understanding the problem as a consequence of the functioning of the system and thus, intervening in the system. In the example below, we observe a change in the food consumption system, obesity being the unwanted result.

The Changing Nutrition Landscape

In 2014, a study led by Imperial College collected data from 186 countries and found that the number of obese people in the world has surpassed that of underweight people. The study identified that the number of obese people rose from 105 million in 1975 to 641 million in 2014, while the number of underweight people also rose, but from 220 million to 462 million over the same period. This change in the nutrition and weight landscape shows the evolution of the system: bad nutrition is no longer just a lack of food and calories, but also the consumption of too many low-nutritive calories. This is a new scenario, emerging from the evolution of a complex system of food consumption.

Once we understand the food consumption system as a set of stakeholders, infrastructure, food product and service supply, regulations, and even cultural and educational factors, we can assume that there has been some change in the structure of the system that has caused its outcomes to change as well. In linear thinking, it could be assumed, for example, that the increased supply of high-calorie and low-nutrient foods, such as ultra-processed foods, may have changed the way people make up their diets, resulting in higher rates of obesity. It is much more likely, however, that such a significant change in outcomes was brought about by a set of system changes, such as regulatory changes, educational changes, changes in food supply and restaurant services, and changes in food production and distribution chains.

As in the example above, public institutions, equipped with their capacities to deal with complicated problems, tend to simplify and order complex issues, removing or attenuating relationships between different actors. This is especially noticeable in the sectoralization of public policies that are closely linked, such as food security and health. This simplification of complex systems prevents public organizations from creating interventions focused on changing dysfunctional systems, often intervening on the consequences or the surface of wicked problems, rather than on their causes.

The systems thinking approach allows public managers to observe the elements of a system, how they interact, and the emergence of systemic outcomes, creating a space of opportunity to address the systemic causes of a wicked problem. This is especially true when these problems are related to the behavior of citizens, who often interact with many elements and make decisions that are based on many factors, rational or not. In this way, systems thinking is a strategy for working with the complexity of systems and behaviors, rather than simply avoiding it.

Summary

1. A system can be defined as an "interconnected set of elements that is organized in order to achieve some goal."
2. From a systems theory point of view, everything known is part of a system and is usually immersed in larger systems.
3. When we look at public policy systems, it is common to observe that there is a large number of and diversity amongst stakeholders, structures, regulations, and technologies, as well as diverse relationships between the parts of these systems. We could define this as a complex system.
4. It is common for governments to assume that the systemic behaviors they want to affect are linear, associated with clear answers to known or knowable questions.
5. When it comes to public policy and social problems, however, we almost always find ourselves in complex systems. Unfortunately, public managers often lack the tools to deal with such complexity.
6. Systems thinking enables public institutions to observe the elements of a system, how they interact, and the emergence of systemic outcomes, creating a space of opportunity to address the systemic causes of a social problem.

Suggested Readings

OECD. "Systems Approaches in the Public Sector: From Theory to Practice." Systems Approaches to Public Sector Challenges, August 11, 2017, 11–39. https://doi.org/10.1787/9789264279865-3-en.

Chen, C. C., and N. Crilly. "A Framework for Complex Design: Lessons from Synthetic Biology." Systemic Design, 2018, 53–67. https://doi.org/10.1007/978-4-431-55639-8_2.

Morin, Edgar. On Complexity. Hampton Press, 2008. https://doi.org/10.1604/9781572738010.

Johnson, S. Emergence. The Connected Lives of Ants, Brains, Cities, and Software, 2001. https://doi.org/10.1604/9780684868752.

Meadows, D. H. Thinking in Systems. A Primer. Chelsea Green Publishing Company, 2008.

Emery, F., and Russel Ackmory. On Purposeful Systems. An Interdisciplinary Analysis of Individual and Social Behavior As a System of Purposeful Events. Routledge, 2006. https://doi.org/10.1604/9780202307985.

Canty-Waldron, Julia. "Using Systems Thinking to Create More Impactful Social Policy." Journal of Futures Studies, December 2019. https://jfsdigital.org/vol-19-no-2-dec-2014/articles-2/using-systems-thinking-to-create-more-impactful-social-policy/.

Foster-Fishman, P. G., B. Nowell, and H. Yang. "Putting the System Back into Systems Change: A Framework for Understanding and Changing Organizational and Community Systems." American Journal of Community Psychology 39, no. 3–4 (May 18, 2007): 197–215. https://doi.org/10.1007/s10464-007-9109-0.

Muturana, H., and F. J. Varela. Autopoiesis and Cognition. The Realization of the Living. No. 42, 1980. https://doi.org/10.1023/b134762.

Senge, P. M. The Fifth Discipline. The Art and Practice of the Learning Organization, 1994.
J. T. Hämäläinen, "Governance Solutions for Wicked Problems: Metropolitan Innovation Ecosystems as Frontrunners to Sustainable Well-Being." Technology Innovation Management Review 5, no. 10 (October 28, 2015): 31–41. https://doi.org/10.22215/timreview/935.
Taysom, E., and N. Crilly. "Resilience in Sociotechnical Systems: The Perspectives of Multiple Stakeholders." She Ji: The Journal of Design, Economics, and Innovation 3, 3 (2017): 165–82. https://doi.org/10.1016/j.sheji.2017.10.011.
Buchanan, R. "Systems Thinking and Design Thinking: The Search for Principles in the World We Are Making." She Ji: The Journal of Design, Economics, and Innovation 5, no. 2 (2019): 85–104. https://doi.org/10.1016/j.sheji.2019.04.001.
Jones, P. "Systemic Design: Design for Complex, Social, and Sociotechnical Systems." Handbook of Systems Sciences, 2020, 1–25. https://doi.org/10.1007/978-981-13-0370-8_60-1.
Jones, P. H. "Systemic Design Principles for Complex Social Systems." Translational Systems Sciences, 2014, 91–128. https://doi.org/10.1007/978-4-431-54478-4_4.

Chapter 6
Embedding Behavioral Diagnostics within Systems Thinking

6.1 Mapping Systems and Subsystems

The process of diagnosing a system is exploratory and not an easy task. When integrating systems thinking with behavioral insights, it is necessary to start from the multiple trajectories of the stakeholders in the system, to understand the complex relationships that form from their interactions, creating a systems model. In practice, this means that the larger the number of stakeholders involved and the more interactions and trajectories we take into account, the more complex the system will be.

One way to diagnose a public policy system is to start with its parts: the agents that make up the system and their behavior. This method allows us to explore the actions of the system's components individually, in order to compose the system as a whole. Starting from the idea that public problems are unwanted outcomes of a system, the first step must be to define them, and then map the systemic mechanism that created them.

Defining a problem and its causes depends on the perspective of the beholder. This is why it is important to be comfortable with provisional definitions, which are always open to revision as we delve deeper into the system we want to act on. In the methodology presented in this book, we will start from the following definition of a problem: an undesirable and observable outcome in a given social setting. A problem definition breaks down in four features:

- It is the **result** of the action of a system, that is, it is a product of a mechanism.
- It is **undesirable**, that is, someone finds that situation uncomfortable.
- It is **observable** and can be perceived by different stakeholders.
- It is found in a **given social setting**, being particular to that reality, even though it bears similarities with problems in other places.

G. Lichand et al., *Behavioral Insights for Policy Design*,
https://doi.org/10.1007/978-3-031-33034-6_6

Case Study: Defining the Problem in the Case of Female Labor Force Participation in Saudi Arabia

To illustrate the methodology, we will use the case of Saudi women's low participation in the workforce, introduced in Chap. 3. If we start from the idea that the problem is an undesired outcome, it is first necessary to describe it more succinctly and specifically in order to demonstrate why it is important. For example:

Economically active women in Saudi Arabia cannot work outside the home without challenging social norms and obtaining the approval of their male "guardians."

This problem presents a **specific setting** (economically active women in Saudi Arabia), an **observable** outcome (they cannot enter the workforce), and an **undesirable** one (without challenging social norms and getting the approval of their male "guardians"). The initial definition of the problem must be open enough to motivate an exploration, but narrow enough to have a focus. Otherwise, it will not be possible to explore reality with necessary attention or curiosity.

Once the public problem has been defined, the next step is to map the systemic mechanism that produces it. To do this, it is necessary to gather information about the problem, the agents involved, and its history. This process also includes listing the hypotheses about how the problem is produced by the system, to be validated through primary or secondary research, such as ethnographic research or literature review.

For hypotheses listing, we seek to discuss the cause-and-effect relationships of the problem at hand. In this way, we are able to confirm or refute the ways in which the nodes of the system are connected, helping us to build a more complete model. It is recommended to go through cycles of refinement of the hypothesis, especially with literature review. The goal is to answer most of the hypotheses with secondary data and apply primary research only for specific and well-defined hypotheses.

Case Study: Defining Hypotheses About the Problem

Returning to the example of the Saudi women presented above, it is possible to raise hypotheses about the cause and effect of the situation:

- Traditional family upbringing in Saudi Arabia prevents girls from having role models of working women.
- Husbands do not accept or approve of their wives working for financial reasons.
- Husbands and fathers are afraid of being looked down upon if their wives and daughters work outside the home.

Each of these hypotheses can be verified through secondary or primary research, helping the team to understand the different systemic mechanisms that produce the public problem being addressed.

The definition of hypotheses allows the key stakeholders involved in the system to be mapped. The stakeholders (or nodes of the system) perform sets of connected actions which make up the system. The list of key stakeholders is built by checking which agent is involved in each hypothesis. Once the hypotheses are confirmed, we can connect the stakeholders in the system. This method does not necessarily seek to define a target audience, since systemic solutions can be designed for various audiences.

It is possible to divide the stakeholders into two sets. The first is the set of direct stakeholders, in other words, those who are directly involved or affected by the mapped problem. The indirect stakeholders are those who are not directly affected by the problem, but who are related to the direct stakeholders. So, it is possible to say that there is a central part of the system and a peripheral part, in which the direct and indirect stakeholders are located, respectively.

Case Study: Mapping Direct and Indirect Stakeholders
Imagining the home situation of Saudi women who are able to work, we can consider them, their male guardians, and immediate family as **direct stakeholders**.

We can think of neighbors, distant family, media communicators, government agents, coworkers, and employers as **indirect stakeholders**.

The next step is data collection, which corresponds to fieldwork and desk research. These two tools allow quantitative and qualitative information to be compiled, helping to verify the hypotheses about the system and generate new insights.

6.1.1 Typical Cases and Positive Deviants

The main goal of the field and desk research is to understand the journeys of the direct stakeholders and how the indirect stakeholders relate to them. This perspective is important because the trajectories of these agents will be essential in composing the system. To systematize a trajectory, a step-by-step journey is mapped for each stakeholder, demonstrating the succession of events they are involved in. The duration of this journey can be a single day (routine) or the life history of that individual.

In primary research, ethnographic tools can be used to collect the life history of the direct stakeholders. The positive deviance approach seeks to generate insights from the analysis of two different types of individuals: the typical cases and the positive deviants. The former refer to people who suffer directly from the problem we want to address in a typical or expected way. The latter are those people who are inserted in the same setting and should suffer from the problem as well, but for some reason manage to solve or avoid the problem. By mapping the trajectories of these two types of individuals, we can identify, by contrast and similarity, how the system behaves and what its key variables are (see Table 6.1).

Table 6.1 Typical case versus positive deviant

Typical case	Positive deviant
Direct stakeholders who experience the challenge directly and suffer from its consequences. These are the people who experience the reality that we want to change. E.g.: Economically active women who are not able to work outside the home and are part of traditional families.	Direct stakeholders similar to the typical case, but who, for some reason, do not suffer from the challenge. They are people who have developed coping strategies or experience another set of factors that prevent them from suffering from the problem. E.g.: Economically active women who work outside the home despite being part of a family that follows traditional social norms.

Source: elaborated by the authors

After the fieldwork, it is necessary to dive into the information generated, to map the different stories that exist in the system, and to connect the trajectories of the stakeholders that make up this system. Interviews with specialists and data research are also important to critically analyze the stories collected. This is because there are conjunctural and structural factors that may not be perceived by the direct stakeholders, but that are still part of the system. It is important to always start with the stakeholders, since they live the concrete reality and generate very important insights for the project, leaving a deeper analysis with specialists to a follow-up analysis.

6.1.2 Personas and Storyboards

To consolidate the stories, it is necessary to group them according to each stakeholder in an attempt to map a *standard story*, that is, one that could explain the trajectory of a group of stakeholders. Possible divergences between the individual stories can be considered, but the most important activity is to synthesize their journey into a common trajectory. Each direct stakeholder should have a standard story for the typical case and a standard story for the positive deviant.

Case Study: Creating Standard Stories

Imagine, for example, that you have collected the stories of ten different typical case families. Based on the secondary research data, it is possible to define the most representative stories and their unifying elements, mapping this standard story step-by-step onto a system.

The positive deviants, on the other hand, are characterized as exceptions to the rule, that is, their stories are successful variations of the standard story. Because of this, these stories add qualitative and comparative value to the system design.

Following the example, consider that, in the typical cases, the male guardians claim that they do not allow women from their families to work for fear of being looked down upon by their neighbors and peers. But for the positive deviants, the opinion of other men matters little, or they do not believe that they will have their reputation tarnished. From this comparison, it is possible to hypothesize that there is peer pressure or a reputation factor that prevents husbands or fathers from allowing women to work outside the home.

Some tools can be used to consolidate stories. The first of these is the persona, a character that represents the behavioral profile of a group of stakeholders. Personas are important in creating a representation of a group from a behavioral point of view. At this point, we can understand the attributes shared by the group, with the goal of drawing an archetypal character. For comparative purposes, different personas can be created for the typical case and for the positive deviants.

Case Study: Creating a Persona for the Typical Case

Designing a persona begins with a story that represents a group of people and their experience with the public problem. Table 6.2 illustrates a persona representing a typical case about women entering the workforce in Saudi Arabia.

Table 6.2 Saudi woman persona

<table>
<tr><td>Demographics
Name: Maryam
Age: 28</td><td colspan="2">Story
Maryam is a 28-year-old woman married to Ahmad. Maryam and her husband were raised in traditional families where no women worked. But recently, the couple has encountered financial problems and Maryam has started to think about getting a job outside of the home. Ahmad, however, believes that women working outside the home are frowned upon.</td></tr>
<tr><td>Goals
To work outside the home.
To help with the family's bills.
To get approval from her husband.</td><td>Obstacles
Possible stain on husband's reputation.
No close family role models.</td><td>Social environment
Financial difficulties.
Traditional family.
Few examples of women working outside the home.</td></tr>
</table>

Source: elaborated by the authors

Following the persona, a storyboard can be created to tell the story of each persona, drawn like a comic book. This tool allows complex situations to be described in a rich yet simple, step-by-step manner, representing multiple stakeholders when necessary. A good storyboard has three to six panels for each situation represented.

Case Study: Building a Storyboard for the Typical Case

If the persona represents a character, the storyboard represents the experience of that character in the system being mapped. The storyboard presented in Table 6.3 describes the domestic dynamics between a typical case woman and her husband when it comes to his resistance to her proposal of working outside the home.

Table 6.3 Typical case storyboard

Scene 1 Maryam and her husband Ahmad are having financial problems.	*Scene 2* To help, Maryam started thinking about working outside the home and saw some job offers for women.	*Scene 3* But Maryam has never worked and does not know any woman that works.
Scene 4 Still, Maryam decided to propose the idea to her husband, hoping to get his approval.	*Scene 5* When she proposed the idea, Ahmad responded that most husbands do not approve of their wives working and that it might be frowned upon by other men.	*Scene 6* Ahmad, although not personally against it, rejects Maryam's idea because he believes that his relatives and peers would not approve of Maryam working outside the home.

Source: elaborated by the authors

Tip
Check the toolkit presented in Chap. 12.

6.1.3 Turning Storyboards into Systems

Mapping a system is a reflective practice: it is necessary to create a map, reflect on it, and refine it. Therefore, it is a process that requires time and patience: the system map will go through an iterative process, generating several versions until it reaches the final form. Storyboards are like system fragments that form the system once combined.

One way to represent system maps is through Causal Loop Diagrams (CLD). These models can show cycles of reinforcement or equilibrium in a system, often explaining the nonlinearity and complexity of the system. These diagrams have their own notation, which we will adopt in this book.

Causal Loop Diagrams are models of systems that allow us to visualize the variables and relationships between them. Understanding a CLD requires careful, guided reading, with special attention to the cycles of the system and the relationships between variables (see Table 6.4).

Table 6.4 Elements of a system

Element	Description	Representation
Variable	It is the node of the system and should be described as something that always increases or decreases, preferably nouns and written in positive form (e.g., engagement rather than disengagement)	It is usually represented with the word that corresponds to the variable.
Positive connection	Represents a connection where the variables go in the same direction, i.e., if A increases, B increases, or if A decreases, B decreases.	A —+→ B
Negative connection	Represents a connection where the variables go in opposite directions, i.e., if A increases, B decreases, or if A decreases, B increases.	A —-→ B
Reinforcing feedback loop	Represents a closed loop that feeds back into the system in the same direction in which it is fed, i.e., it is a self-reinforcing loop.	(R)
Balancing feedback loop	Represents a closed loop that feedbacks to the system in the opposite direction in which it is fed, i.e., it is an equilibrium loop.	(B)

Source: elaborated by the authors

Rarely is a system self-explanatory, that is, rarely can a system be read without supporting materials. This is because contextual information, such as the problems that the system generates or the function that the system performs, is fundamental to a deeper analysis. Moreover, a CLD is a model, that is, a cutout of the real world – although this model still contains some complexity, it does not faithfully portray the complexity of reality, albeit closer than linear models.

Reading a System from the CLD (Causal Loop Diagram)
A pedagogical way to exercise the reading of a CLD system is through examples. Recently, a discussion has taken over the world of public management: the productivity of public servants. In a world with fewer resources and more complex problems, the government's performance has been demanding more from the people who make up the government's technical and political bodies. These rapid changes clash with a bureaucratic structure that builds on stability and predictability, generating heated discussions about work ethics in the public service.

This situation affects the day-to-day work of civil servants. With few resources, complex governance, and bureaucratic constraints, many civil servants deal with increasing demands at work by increasing their productivity. The most productive ones are recognized through leading positions in their teams, taking on leadership roles or particularly challenging projects.

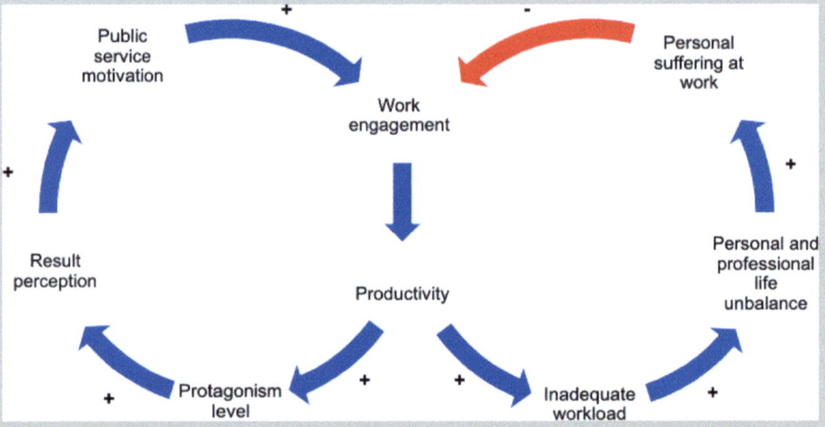

Fig. 6.1 Causal Loop Diagram (CLD) of public servant's motivation. (Source: elaborated by the authors)

Perceiving the results of this work and recognition, these employees feel more motivated and, consequently, increase their work engagement and productivity. This cycle continuously reinforces itself, i.e., the more engaged the employee, the better results they subsequently produce, heightening their motivation to engage further in the work, and so on.

This cycle, however, cannot reinforce itself forever: other issues soon come into play that regulate the cycle of productivity and engagement. Once the workload exceeds the limit of the servant's capacity, he may devote most of his time to work, leaving aside other dimensions of his life. An imbalance like this can lead to illness at work, such as burnout problems, decreasing work engagement. As their workload and stress increase, their motivation diminishes, generating a balancing relationship.

The story told by CLD in fig. 6.1 is as follows: a reinforcing cycle and a balancing cycle that oppose each other in defining engagement and productivity in public service work. These cycles, known as feedback loops, are essential concepts for understanding CLD. These components are closed loops feeding back into the system with different polarities.

6.1.3.1 Reinforcing Feedback Loops

Reinforcing loops are cycles that feed back in the same direction. That is, they are self-reinforcing cycles which create conditions for their variables to amplify. In the story of engagement, the positive cycle is of motivation and engagement: the greater the results achieved by the employee, the greater their motivation will be, increasing their engagement, productivity, and, finally, improving their results – starting the cycle all over again. These loops are responsible for exponential growth in systems, generating crises, instabilities, and even self-destruction. Commonly, to avoid these uncontrolled effects, many systems also rely on balancing cycles.

6.1.3.2 Balancing Feedback Loops

Balancing or equilibrium loops are those that feedback in the opposite way. These loops act as balancing agents in systems, bringing about a dynamic equilibrium. In the example above, work-related illness affects engagement in the opposite way. That is, the greater the productivity and imbalance in professional and personal life, the greater the work-related illness and the lower the engagement. In this way, this balancing cycle counteracts the cycle of motivation, generating a limit for the entire system in terms of engagement and productivity.

6.2 Building the Map

Before designing a system, it is necessary to extract the variables from the stories. This process requires a careful reading of the mapped stories of the key stakeholders in a bid to extract the variables necessary to build the system. At this point, it is recommended to look for as many variables as possible, even if you are not going to use them all. Table 6.5 presents an example of a stage of a story and possible variables that can be extracted from such an excerpt.

Variables are the nodes of the system and are mapped as we better understand how the system works and its parts interact. When naming variables, a few tips are important:

Table 6.5 Turning information into variables

"Ahmad, although not personally against it, rejects Maryam's idea because he believes that his relatives and peers do not approve of Maryam working outside the home."

Excerpt	Variable
"Not personally against it"	Personal approval of husbands
"Rejects"	de facto approval of husbands
"Believes that his relatives and peers do not approve"	Perceived social disapproval
"Maryam working outside the home"	Women in the labor force

Source: elaborated by the authors

- **Name variables as quantities that can vary**. The dynamic aspect of CLD means especially the changes in variables, as they rise or fall, grow or decline.
- **Use nouns**. Verbs and actions are conveyed in the arrows, so they should be avoided.
- **Separate perceptions from actual states.** Sometimes, it is useful to include perceptions on the CLD, but they should be signaled to clarify the variables in the diagrams.

Tip
Check the toolkit presented in Chap. 12.

After the survey of variables, it is time to connect them. It is important to have a critical look at the possible connections, trying to verify if the variables really have a direct cause-and-effect relationship. This careful connection is important to be made because a system with many connections can look more like a tangle of lines than a CLD.

From this point on, the small blocks or subsystems that make up the CLD begin to emerge. The task now is to connect them together (see Fig. 6.2), like putting together a puzzle – how can these pieces of the system be connected? Are there missing pieces? Are there repeated variables in different subsystems that demonstrate a point of convergence?

When putting together a system, it is common for it to be large and very complex. The post-assembly analysis of the system allows it to be simplified based on the answer to the question "what story am I trying to tell?" Like any story, if we give unnecessary details we lose didactics and focus, but if we give few details we omit important aspects. The same system can tell several stories and they can be framed in many ways, but they must still be clear and direct.

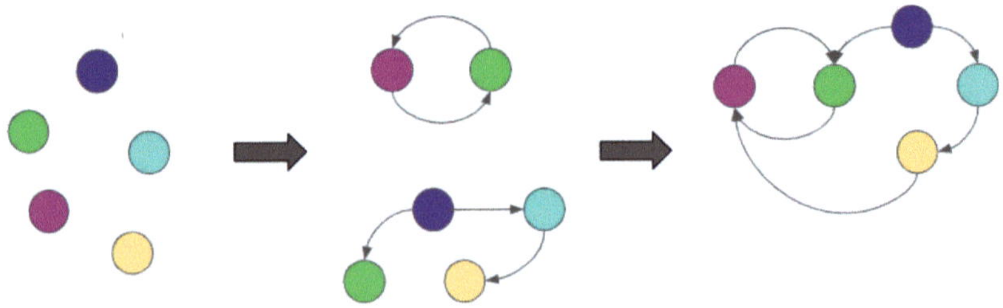

Fig. 6.2 Building a Causal Loop Diagram. (Source: elaborated by the authors)

Case Study: Building the CLD

The first step in assembling the systemic map is to link the direct causality variables. In Fig. 6.3, we list the variables mapped from the storyboard of the typical case and connect the variables depicting tentative causal relationships.

According to the relationships detailed in Fig. 6.3:

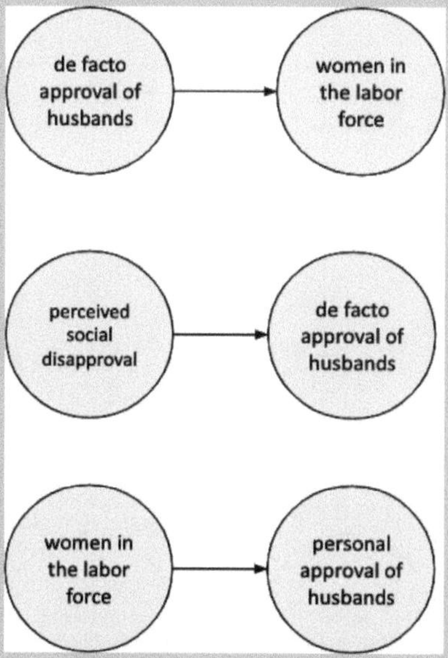

Fig. 6.3 Connecting variables. (Source: elaborated by the authors)

De facto approval of husbands affects the quantity of women in the labor force

- Perceived disapproval affects husbands' de facto approval.
- Women in the labor force affect their husbands' de facto approval.

For each of these relationships, it is possible to qualify the connection between the variables as positive (they relate in the same direction) or negative (they relate in opposite directions), as shown in Fig. 6.4.

Once these qualifications have been made, the statements change:

- The greater the perceived de facto approval of husbands, the greater the number of women in the labor force.
- The greater the perceived disapproval, the lower the de facto approval of husbands/the lower the perceived disapproval, the greater the de facto approval of husbands.
- The more women in the labor force, the greater the level of personal approval among husbands.

You can see that, in some relationships, some variables are repeated. These repetitions allow a puzzle to be put together (see Fig. 6.5).

Fig. 6.4 Qualifying connections. (Source: elaborated by the authors)

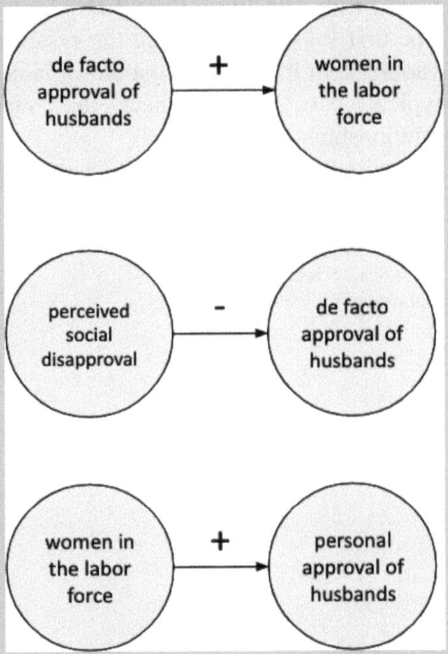

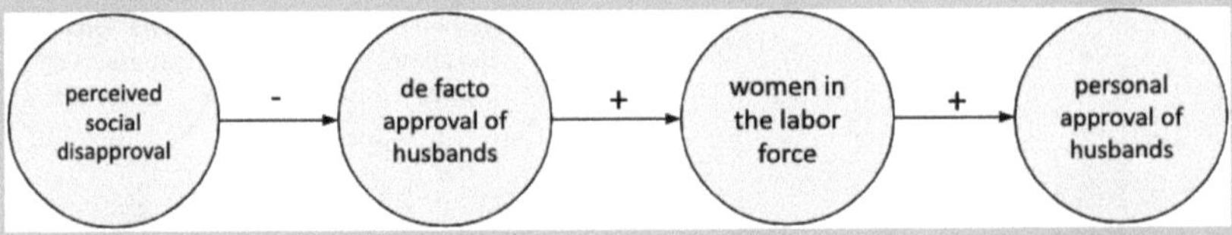

Fig. 6.5 Structuring cause-and-effect relationships. (Source: elaborated by the authors)

Assuming that the personal approval of husbands and de facto approval of husbands tend to be consistent, we can connect the two variables with a positive sign, creating a reinforcing cycle, as shown in Fig. 6.6.

The small system in Fig. 6.6 **demonstrates a self-reinforcing cycle being limited by a variable. Through these linked relationships, we can describe the following story:**

"The more husbands approve of women working outside the home, the more women enter the labor force, reinforcing husbands' personal approval of work outside the home and increasing the chances of husbands actually approving of their wives' work. Meanwhile, the perceived social disapproval of women's work decreases the chances of husbands' approval."

This small system shows a play of forces between the husband's personal approval, the amount of women in the labor force, and the perception of social disapproval, which acts as a limiter to the reinforcement cycle drawn in Fig. 6.6.

Tip

Check the toolkit presented in Chap. 12.

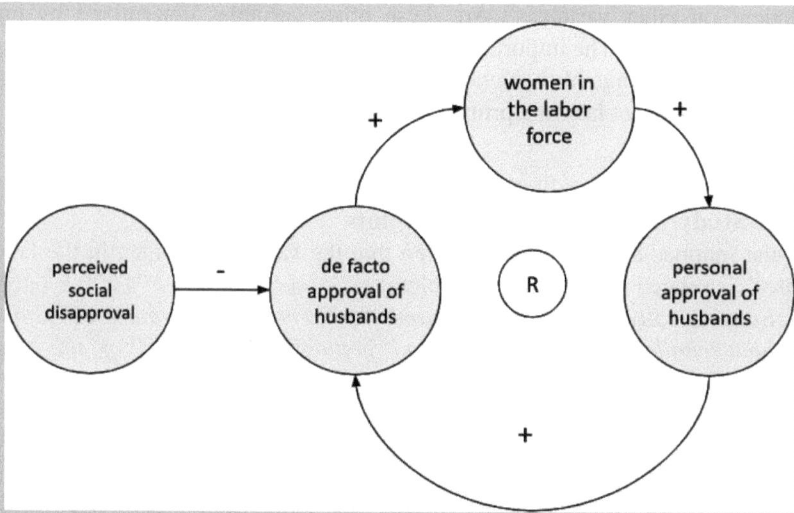

Fig. 6.6 Finding the loops. (Source: elaborated by the authors)

6.3 Identifying Leverage Points

When we analyze a system,we soon realize that the cause-consequence logic is circular, not linear. This change in perspective allows us to understand how problems persist over time and the importance of interrupting the cycle that we think is problematic. One of the ways to find opportunities to interrupt cycles and promote change is by finding the system's leverage points. These are localized opportunities for intervention that generate changes throughout the system – it is like finding your Achilles heel, where a small action can generate much larger effects.

Often, when we intervene in a system, we seek to alleviate the problems, that is, the products of the system. Such work, however, often serves only to reduce the damage. Delving deeper into the mechanism of the system enables us to search for the causes that initiate a vicious cycle, or the factors that limit a virtuous cycle. Working at this point in the system allows greater "leverage" to intervene in the cycles, providing opportunity for a more significant systemic change than simply treating the consequences.

The points of intervention in a system are rarely obvious. To find them, we start with an analysis of the points at which the people involved can change key behaviors from an intervention, be it a product, service, or communication piece. By determining the intervention point, we create possibilities of solutions that can be prototyped and tested to generate public programs or even compose a government action already in action.

To find the leverage points, search the system for the variables that have the greatest influence in generating the problem we want to tackle. Is this variable dependent on other variables? Are these other variables determined by human choices or behavior? The important thing here is to find where in the system the key stakeholder can change his behaviors in order to generate consequences throughout the system that affect how the problem is created.

Case Study: Identifying Leverage Points

In the mapped system, it can be seen that the variable "women in the labor force" is related to the defined problem:

Economically active women in Saudi Arabia cannot work outside the home without challenging the norms and getting the approval of the male "guardians."

Thus, the variable "women in the labor force" cannot be the leverage point. Looking at the rest of the system, we can see that the reinforcing cycle can be vicious (the less husbands approve, the less women participate in the market) or virtuous (the more husbands approve, the more women participate in the market). The factor external to the cycle, "perceived social disapproval" can determine the path the cycle takes (see Fig. 6.7). Thus, it is a relevant leverage point in the system, with the potential to influence husbands' behavior and generate systemic change.

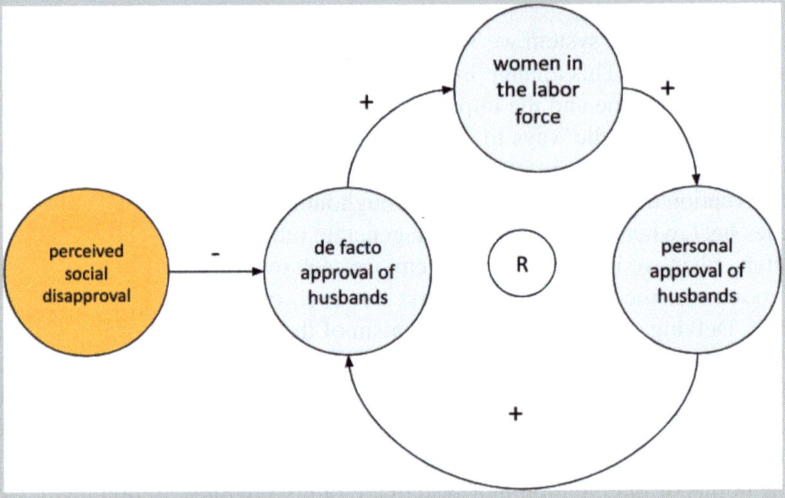

Fig. 6.7 Finding a lever to work on. (Source: elaborated by the authors)

Summary

1. This chapter presented an approach to embed behavioral diagnostics in systems thinking.
2. Through a design approach, we focused on the stakeholders' experiences to understand a situation and create journeys or trajectories of these agents within the system.
3. This approach allows for less abstraction, focusing on observable events to map variables, an essential and yet difficult part of system mapping.
4. By transforming trajectories in variables, it is possible to speculate about the quality of their relations and find reinforcing or balancing feedback loops.
5. Once the system is mapped, leverage points can be identified, highliting opportunities for public interventions.
6. In later chapters, we will see that behavioral diagnostics embedded in systems thinking allows practitioners to identify plausible and feasible behaviorally-informed interventions, i.e., those with real potential to create systems-level change.

Suggested Readings

Bursztyn, Leonardo, Gonzales Alessandra, and Yanagizawa-Drott, David (2020) "Misperceived Social Norms: Female Labor Force Participation in Saudi Arabia", The American Economic Review, v. 110 (10), pp. 2997-3029.

Hanington, B., & Martin, B. (2019). Universal methods of design expanded and revised. Rockport Publishers.

Kim, D. H. (1999). Introduction to systems thinking. Pegasus communications, Inc.

Liedtka, J., & Ogilvie, T. (2011). Designing for growth: A design thinking toolkit for managers. Columbia University Press.

Luhmann, N., Baecker, D., & Gilgen, P. (2021). Introduction to systems theory. Polity.

Pascale, R. T., Sternin, J., & Sternin, M. (2010). The power of positive deviance: How unlikely innovators solve the world's toughest problems. Harvard Business Press.

Chapter 7
Augmenting the Public Management Toolkit with Behavioral Insights: The PRIx Framework

7.1 Introduction

This chapter offers a methodology for augmenting the public manager's toolkit with the behavioral mechanisms discussed in the previous chapters. This methodology, the **PRIx framework**, is an acronym for pricing, regulatory, and information policies, whereby the *x* indicates its use combined with the behavioral mechanisms of the MSI framework. In a nutshell, the framework aims at repurposing policy instruments already widely used in the public sector, modifying them to account for the motivation, self-control, and inattention problems that affect the "real citizen."

In some cases, small changes to existing policies are sufficient to activate behavioral mechanisms that were previously not accounted for, as we will see in the following sections. In other cases, the PRIx framework suggests surprising approaches – including the formulation of policies that seem to escape traditional policy tools altogether. In all cases, the application of the PRIx framework can enable progress even in the face of social problems that have resisted multiple public sector interventions, by offering a fresh look at old dilemmas.

7.2 Traditional Uses of Policy Tools

To start, let us characterize what we call the traditional uses of some policy tools widely used in the public sector to correct externalities and to mitigate social inequalities. The goal is to describe these tools as typically designed for "ideal citizens," as a means of contrasting them to the policy tools augmented by behavioral insights (which we will introduce in the sections that follow), designed with "real citizens" at their core.

G. Lichand et al., *Behavioral Insights for Policy Design*,
https://doi.org/10.1007/978-3-031-33034-6_7

7.2.1 Pricing Policies

Changing prices to incentivize or discourage private behaviors with public consequences is perhaps the most obvious example of a public policy tool designed for the "ideal citizen." The target audience are precisely those who respond to financial costs and benefits with unlimited attention to the expected returns of each alternative, absent internal conflicts between rationality and affect, immune to social pressure, and with perfect ability to follow through on past plans.

In the case of products and services directly controlled by the government (such as oil and utility prices, in some countries), prices can be changed directly. For instance, at the time Petrobrás was a State-owned oil company, if the Brazilian government wanted to discourage the use of private vehicles, it could have the company directly raise fuel prices. With higher prices, the ideal citizen would consume less fuel – either by driving less or by switching from driving to public transit. To give another example, if a government wants to encourage credit intake, it can have public banks lower interest rates faced by consumers. The ideal citizen would respond to lower interest rates by saving less and/or borrowing more.

In most cases, however, prices can only be influenced indirectly, through taxes or subsidies. If a government wants to decrease the consumption of alcoholic beverages, to return to our previous example, it can introduce a tax – which tends to increase prices for the final consumer. The ideal citizen would consume less alcohol when its price increases. Alternatively, if a government wants to increase the use of fertilizers by smallholder farmers, it could offer subsidies specifically targeted at this group, for example, through vouchers that could be used to redeem discounts on the purchase of productive inputs in specialized stores (in a model in which the government later compensates the stores for the vouchers received). This same model has been popularized in some countries around the world to facilitate access to private education by low-income families. In both cases, the ideal citizen would respond to lower prices by increasing consumption (of fertilizer and of private education, in each case).

Even though economic incentives are powerful, behavioral mechanisms tend to decrease their effectiveness for correcting externalities, and even to make them more regressive when it comes to their impacts on social inequalities. Lack of intrinsic motivation to adopt a certain behavior, social pressure not to adopt it, inconsistencies between plans and actions, and inattention to prices, all tend to make the "real citizen" much less responsive to price changes promoted directly or indirectly by the government. Even worse, under inattention and cognitive load, the incidence of taxes (subsidies) might fall more (less) on the poor.

7.2.2 Regulatory Policies

Another tool routinely used by public managers are regulations that prohibit or enforce certain behaviors with public consequences. If a government wants to discourage cigarette smoking, it can, for instance, prohibit smoking in public places. If it wants to restrict the risks associated with vehicle accidents, it can mandate wearing seat belts.

Since violating prohibitions or mandates is generally associated with financial punishments (with direct costs, in the case of fines, or indirect costs, in the case of arrests), the logic of regulatory policies approaches that of pricing policies when it comes to the mechanisms through which they are able to incentivize or discourage behaviors. After all, in the absence of these direct and/or indirect costs, such regulations would be totally ineffective – at least from the perspective of the "ideal citizen," who compares the expected financial costs and benefits of complying with regulation or not. As such, the discussion on the effectiveness and distributional impacts of prices, taxes, and subsidies applies just the same to regulatory policies too. Accounting for the behavioral mechanisms that affect the "real citizen," these instruments tend to be less effective and more regressive than typically anticipated by policymakers.

7.2.3 Information Policies

Information campaigns are also widely used in the public sector to promote or discourage behaviors with public consequences. If a government wants to encourage vaccination, it can publicize the expected risks of not getting immunized, as well as heavily publicize the wide availability of immunization clinics. Alternatively, if a government wants to discourage corruption amongst public officials, it can publicize channels through which citizens can report it, as well as the consequences for public servants found guilty.

In both cases, these tools can be understood as means to clarify the expected financial costs or benefits of the behaviors in question. In this sense, once again, the discussion about the effectiveness of prices, taxes, and subsidies to correct externalities and promote distributive justice applies to information policies too. Behavioral mechanisms that affect "real citizens" tend to make these campaigns less effective than expected.

7.3 Augmented Tools to Address Motivation Problems

Next, we will discuss how to augment public policy tools with behavioral insights from the MSI framework when it comes to motivation problems of the "real citizen." Concretely, we will focus on how pricing, regulatory, and information policies could be modified by these insights to activate intrinsic motivation, social pressure, or social image concerns, above and beyond their effects on expected financial costs and benefits.

7.3.1 Pricing Policies

Intrinsic Motivation

Prices, taxes, and subsidies can also be used to allude to identity, culture, or religion. The rationale behind this alternative use of these traditional tools lies in an innovative way to frame policy changes. Concretely, consider a new subsidy for fertilizer purchases (see Fig. 7.1). The subsidy could be advertised as if it were designed specifically for smallholder farmers – even if, in fact, all farmers are eligible for it. Framing the subsidy this way might lead some smallholder farmers to perceive productive investments as a defining element of their identity, boosting fertilizer purchases far beyond what we would expect solely based on its lower financial costs (thanks to the subsidy).

Alternatively, consider a new tax on alcoholic beverages. Featuring religious leaders in the campaign announcing this new tax might lead alcohol consumption to decrease far beyond what we would expect solely based on its now higher financial costs (thanks to the tax). The reason is that framing the tax this way might lead some of those affiliated with those religions to associate alcohol purchases with violating values that are important to their internal belief system.

Social Expectations

Similarly, prices, taxes, and subsidies can affect social expectations beyond their financial counterparts. Returning to an example discussed in previous chapters, introducing a fine for parents who showed up late to pick up their children from day care ended up making tardiness worse (see Fig. 7.2). The reason is that the fine, presumably, deflated the social costs associated with the undesirable behavior by putting a price tag on tardiness ("monetizing" guilt). Ignoring social punishments and rewards prevented the fine from achieving its expected outcomes; on the contrary, it magnified the prevalence of the undesirable behavior.

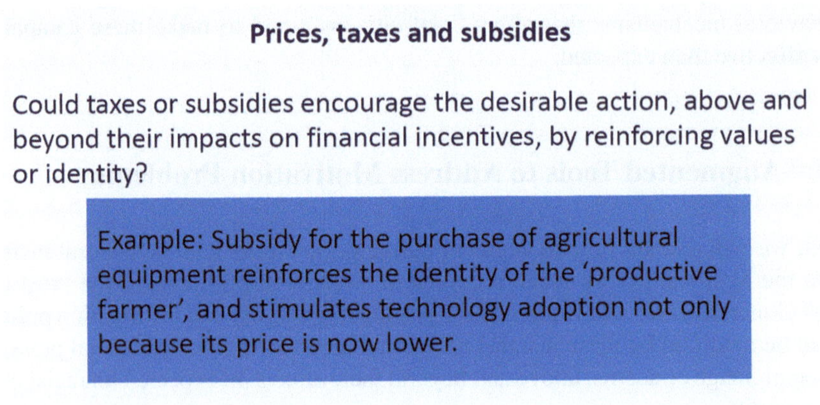

Fig. 7.1 Pricing policies vs. intrinsic motivation. (Source: elaborated by the authors)

In addition to monitoring possible unanticipated consequences of pricing policies on social expectations, public managers can try to use this mechanism to their advantage. For instance, introducing a surcharge for those who consume water or electricity above their neighbors' average consumption can activate social expectations that end up inducing everyone to lower consumption. That might be the case even if each citizen's consumption levels are not public knowledge. If that were the case, water and electricity consumption might decrease far beyond what we would expect solely based on its now higher financial costs (thanks to the surcharge).

Social Image Concerns

Prices, taxes, and subsidies can also activate social image concerns. In the context of the surcharge on water or electricity consumption just discussed, if individual consumption levels were visible to the neighbors, that might lead consumption to fall by even more, as documented by several studies on the role of social image concerns in such contexts.

Other examples include scholarships or educational awards to encourage good academic standing. Such pricing policies have clear expected effects on student effort among "ideal citizens." Far beyond its incentive effects, however, exposing awardees on "honor rolls" may trigger social rewards, amplifying the effects of these financial benefits, or, conversely, might ultimately backfire for certain students – who want to avoid behaviors that might associate them to groups whom they do not want to identify with.

Having said that, combining pricing instruments with public recognition might help attribute new meaning to good academic standing among certain groups. As we have discussed, studies in the United States document that some high school students of color actively try to avoid a higher GPA when their grades are public, so as not to be associated with white students. In this context, financial awards could help

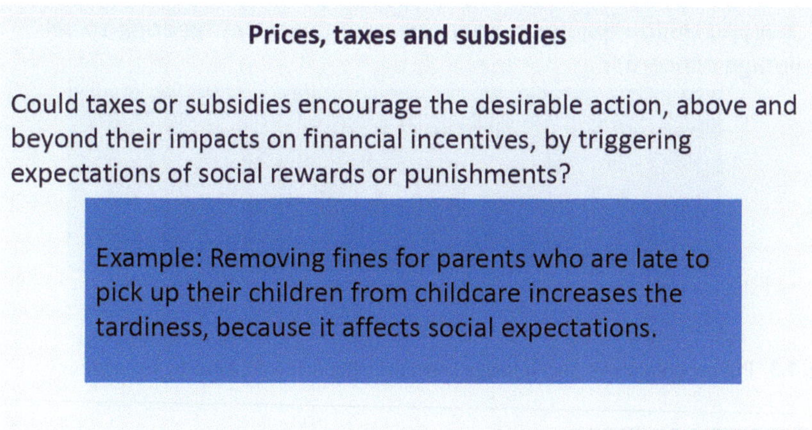

Fig. 7.2 Pricing policies vs. social expectations. (Source: elaborated by the authors)

break down the association between race and academic performance, or that between academic performance and social desirability (or lack thereof).

Financial incentives can also be combined with social image to induce collective action. A recent competition between German schools motivated by the challenge of planting a billion trees[1] demonstrates the power of social pressure, especially in face of collective action (see Fig. 7.3). Publicly recognizing the schools whose students planted the largest numbers of trees triggers in-group behavior on top of leveraging social image concerns. One can imagine that a prize or subsidy for collective action could further stimulate this behavior, far beyond its direct effect on economic incentives.

7.3.2 *Regulatory Policies*

Intrinsic Motivation

Regulatory policies can also allude to values, identity, or culture. In some countries, it is forbidden to sell water or to charge interest on loans. Such prohibitions are often motivated by religious reasons. When most people in a country or a region adopt a certain behavior, identity mechanisms tend to amplify the effects of these regulations, even if the financial penalties associated with violating them are not very high.

Another powerful regulatory policy is setting standards. Standards create social costs for those who challenge them – even in the absence of explicit financial costs

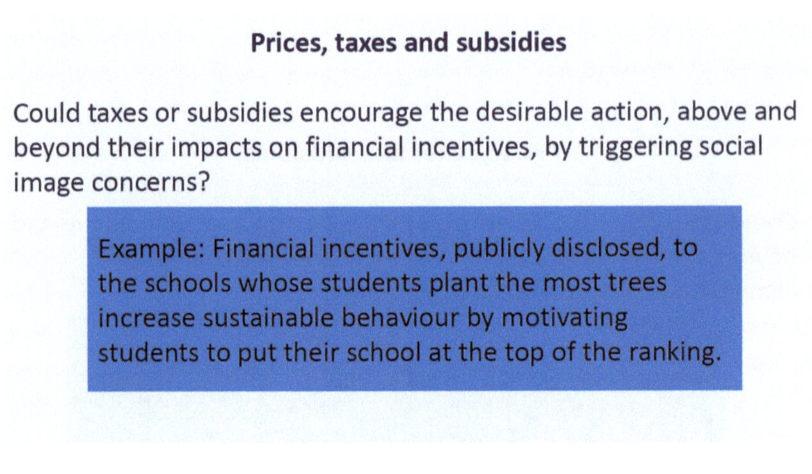

Fig. 7.3 Pricing policies vs. social image concerns. (Source: elaborated by the authors)

[1] Read more: https://believe.earth/en/felix-finkbeiner-planting-trees-and-ideas/ and also https://www.huffpost.com/entry/tree-planting-felix-finkbeiner_n_5ab3b850e4b0decad0478b8c

to those who do not conform. For instance, consider someone who shows up without a tie to a black-tie event. Violating the dress code will force him to walk back home, buy a new tie, or change his plans – each of those imposing financial costs to a greater or lesser extent (at the very least in terms of the opportunity cost of his time). Above and beyond financial costs, however, violating standards can activate emotional costs linked to intrinsic motivations. Returning to an earlier example, when the default option is to be an organ donor, going against that option may trigger an internal conflict of values that ultimately reinforces that option, even in the absence of financial incentives to do so. After all, if being an organ donor was set as the default option, by picking the alternative the individual puts him or herself in the difficult situation of having actively choose not to be a donor.

Setting new standards can also activate values that reinforce adherence to desirable behaviors. For instance, making crop insurance the default option – through the so-called "opt-out model," whereby individuals have to actively choose to uncheck a box if they do not want to take it up, as opposed to the "opt-in model" – can redefine insurance take-up as a defining element of smallholder farmer's identity (see Fig. 7.4). If that were the case, then merely changing standards (to make the take-up of crop insurance the default option) would boost insurance uptake even in the absence of any difference in its financial costs or benefits across the opt-in and opt-out models.

Social Expectations

Regulatory policies can also activate social expectations (see Fig. 7.5). In the examples of selling water or charging interest on loans, as in many other cases, the mere existence of these norms induces beliefs about typical group behavior – even if the behavior itself is not easily observable. Concretely, setting official bands for water or electricity consumption (e.g., "low," "medium," and "high") can reduce consumption merely by inducing citizens to believe that most of their neighbors are in lower consumption bands (see Fig. 7.6).

Social Image Concerns

Public visibility tends to magnify the social forces that shape the behavior of the "real citizen," also in the case of regulatory policies. In the previous example, publicizing individual consumption (or even just the distribution of households within each band, across different neighborhoods) might unlock further reductions in water and electricity consumption by triggering social image concerns.

Setting new standards may even end up generating counterintuitive outcomes, by assigning new meaning to social expectations. Back to our example of students who cut down on effort not to be associated with other social groups, lowering the passing grade – which amounts to setting a new standard – may help to break down the association between GPA and race and, surprisingly, end up encouraging disadvantaged students to study harder (with social image concerns no longer curbing the motivation of students of color to study harder, if the policy change works).

Norms, defaults, mandates and bans

Could mandating or banning an action (including changing the default choice) encourage the desirable action, by reinforcing values or identity?

Example: Making insurance take-up the default choice (e.g., through an opt-out model) increases its coverage by redefining insurance as a part of every farmer's identity.

Fig. 7.4 Regulatory policies vs. intrinsic motivation. (Source: elaborated by the authors)

Norms, defaults, mandates and bans

Could mandating or banning an action (including changing the default choice) encourage the desirable action, by triggering expectations of social rewards or punishments?

Example: Shortening the time buffer until when one can be late to pick up their kid from childcare (e.g., from 15 to 5 minutes) can decrease the tardiness even without changing the fine, by signaling that tardiness is not socially accepted.

Fig. 7.5 Regulatory policies vs. social expectations. (Source: elaborated by the authors)

7.3.3 Information Policies

Intrinsic Motivation

Information campaigns can also activate value, culture, and identity mechanisms. This should come as no surprise: advertisers are masters at associating the consumption of certain products with self-image. Beer and cigarette advertisements have been notorious for trying to attach an image of success to those patronizing their products – rather than communicating accurate information about the expected costs or benefits of their consumption. This only changed when these kind of ads were banned by federal agencies like the US Food and Drug Administration (FDA).

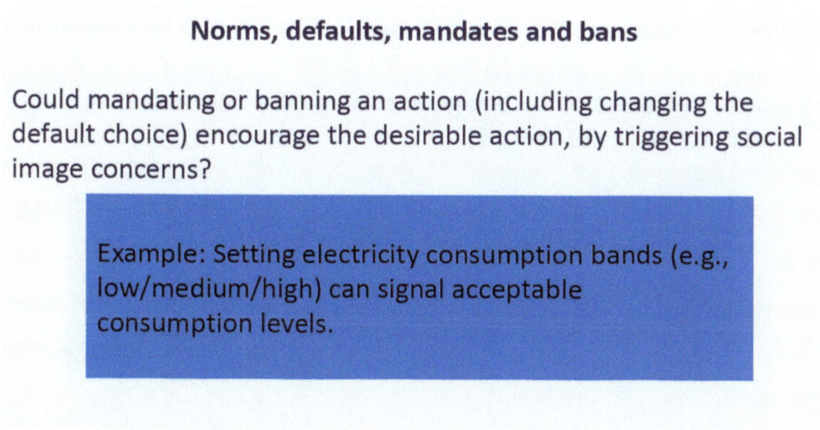

Fig. 7.6 Regulatory policies vs. social image concerns. (Source: elaborated by the authors)

Besides recognizing the potential effects of these ad campaigns in order to regulate them appropriately, public managers can also leverage such potential to promote desirable behaviors or to discourage undesirable behaviors with public consequences.

This holds for almost all of the examples we have dealt with so far: whenever we imagine that prices or regulation could indirectly activate intrinsic motivation mechanisms, campaigns could do this directly. To take just one example, a fertilizer campaign that successfully conveys the idea that a farmer who uses productive inputs is a successful farmer ultimately appeals to their values or their sense of identity (see Fig. 7.7).

Social Expectations

Naturally, information campaigns can also activate social rewards and punishments. As in the previous discussion, whenever prices or regulation could indirectly activate social expectations, campaigns could do this directly.

Back to our example of parents who were systematically late to pick up their children from day care, a campaign illustrating how their tardiness ends up eating away from the time day care staff members have to spend with their own children could activate social punishment mechanisms, thanks to its strong empathetic appeal (see Fig. 7.8). This might be true even if each parent's tardiness is not visible to other parents; hence, even in the absence of social image concerns.

In turn, effective information campaigns to eliminate inaccurate social expectations can be even simpler. It might suffice to survey a representative sample of the population about their private attitudes towards the behavior of interest (regardless of what others think or do), and then share the results (without disclosing their identities) with that target population.

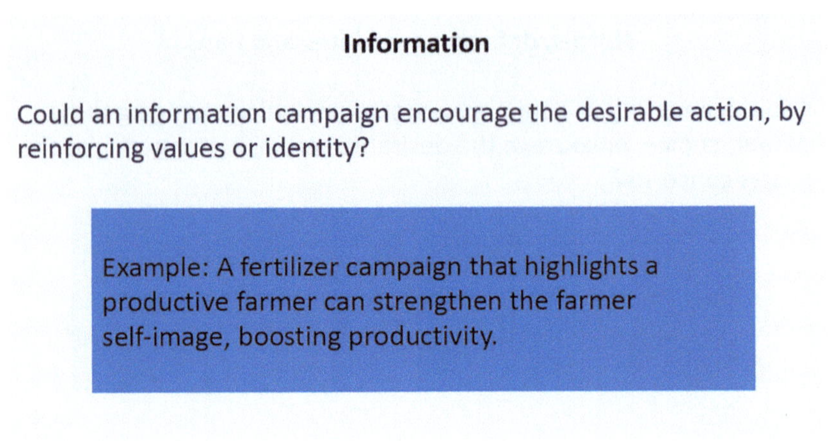

Fig. 7.7 Information policies vs. intrinsic motivation. (Source: elaborated by the authors)

Social Image Concerns

Last, information campaigns can also activate social image concerns (see Fig. 7.9). Once again, whenever prices or regulation could indirectly activate this mechanism, campaigns could do it directly.

Information Campaigns Meet Social Image Concerns

Back to our example of how social image concerns detract from school effort among high school students from disadvantaged backgrounds in the USA, no longer disclosing GPAs publicly would correspond to dismantling an information campaign. After all, choosing what to communicate and what to leave out is also a public policy instrument.

Decreasing the visibility of certain behaviors (here, the outcomes of school effort) tends to be a powerful mechanism to discourage undesirable behaviors motivated by social pressure, above and beyond the example at hand.

Read more:

Bursztyn, Leonard, e Robert Jensen, How Does Peer Pressure Affect Educational Investments? The Quarterly Journal of Economics, Volume 130, Issue 3, August 2015, Pages 1329–1367.

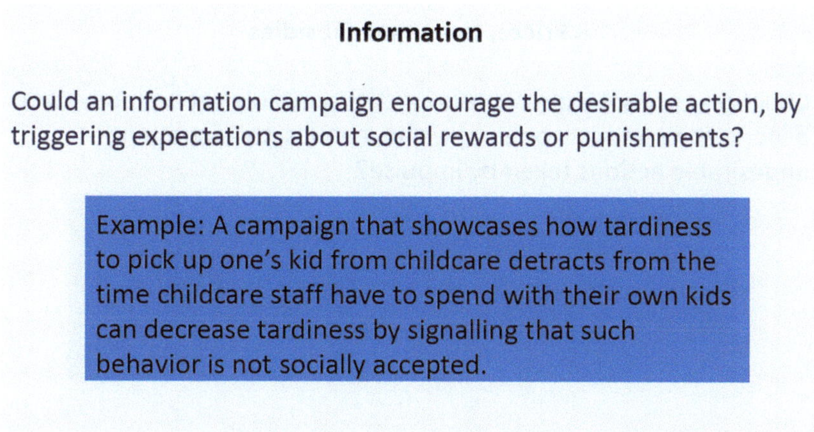

Fig. 7.8 Information policies vs. social expectations. (Source: elaborated by the authors)

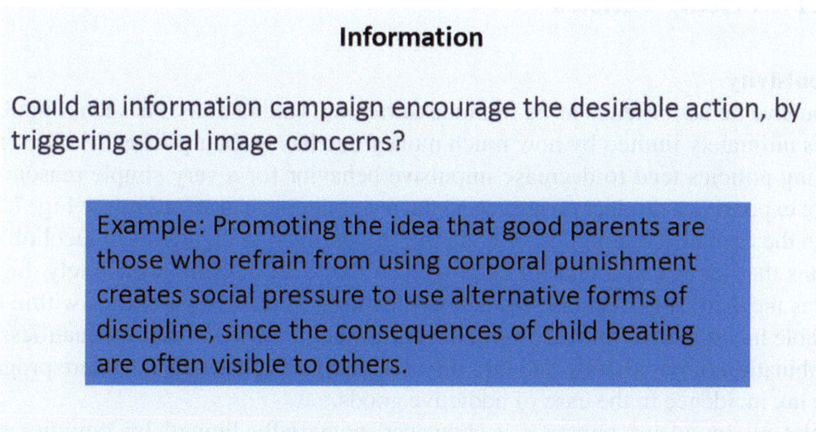

Fig. 7.9 Information policies vs. social image concerns. (Source: elaborated by the authors)

7.4 Augmented Tools to Address Self-Control Problems

Next, we will discuss how to augment public policy tools with behavioral insights from the MSI framework when it comes to self-control problems of the "real citizen." Concretely, we will focus on how pricing, regulatory, and information policies could be modified by these insights to mitigate the consequences of impulsivity, procrastination, or limiting mental models, above and beyond their effects on expected financial costs and benefits.

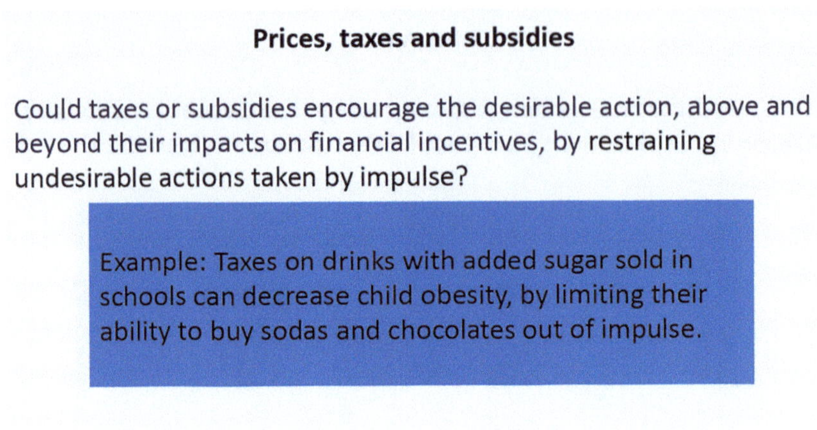

Fig. 7.10 Pricing policies vs. impulsivity. (Source: elaborated by the authors)

7.4.1 Pricing Policies

Impulsivity

Impulsive behavior tends to be immune to rational calculations. As such, impulsivity is ultimately limited by how much money one has in their pocket. In this sense, pricing policies tend to decrease impulsive behavior for a very simple reason: the more expensive a product or service is, the fewer people can afford it (see Fig. 7.10).

In the case of consumption of addictive goods, such as cigarettes or alcohol, this means that taxes could end up helping even the "real citizen." Concretely, higher prices mechanically decrease the scope for fitting impulsive purchases within disposable income. This may end up also contributing to lower social inequalities: the combination of impulsivity and liquidity constraints might result in a more progressive tax incidence in the case of addictive goods.

Not all impulsive behavior is, however, potentially limited by liquidity constraints. Violence and some other forms of crime often bear intimate connections to impulsivity. Since, as previously discussed, cognitive load often limits the ability to exercise self-control, in these cases the poor are more vulnerable to the consequences of impulsive behaviors. Addressing such behaviors requires policy tools that are far more complex than pricing policies can offer.

Procrastination

Discounts or subsidies to decrease future costs tend to be inefficient for dealing with intertemporal inconsistencies. The problem is that individuals suffering from present bias tend to be overly optimistic about their future ability to tolerate these costs.

For this reason, future costs are not the problem (while they remain in the future). Rather, the problem is concentrated on the present costs associated with the desirable behavior – perceived as disproportionately greater than its future benefits. As such, it is discounts or subsidies linked to current expenditures that can be powerful tools to stimulate the desirable behavior in the presence of intertemporal inconsistencies.

Discounts Meet Procrastination

A study in Kenya documented that, when it comes to discounts for purchasing fertilizer, the timing is of essence. When discounts were offered right after harvest, purchases were much higher – even if fertilizer would be delivered only far in the future, by the time of the following planting season. In contrast, future discounts, with payments made in installments over an extended period of time, barely affected fertilizer uptake (see Fig. 7.11).

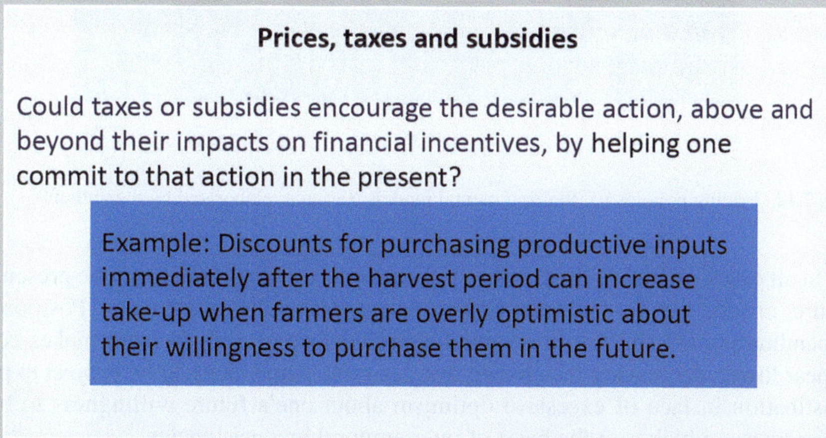

Fig. 7.11 Pricing policies vs. procrastination. (Source: elaborated by the authors)

Another study also in Kenya found that delaying crop insurance payments to the future – in fact, making them conditional on a successful harvest (an arrangement possible when the market is concentrated on a single buyer, as is the case for sugarcane in certain regions of Kenya), substantially increased insurance uptake relative to a discount in the spot price of insurance.

Read more:

Duflo, Ester, Michael Kremer and Jonathan Robinson, Nudging Farmers to Use Fertilizer: Theory and Experimental Evidence from Kenya, The American Economic Review, 101(6), October 2011, pp. 2350–90.

CASABURI, Lorenzo, and Jack WILLIS (2018) "Time Vs. State Insurance: Experimental Evidence From Contract Farming in Kenya", The American Economic Review, 108(2), pp. 3778–3813.

Along those lines, offering discounts to parents who re-enroll their children in private school before the end of the school year could be an effective strategy to reduce dropouts by augmenting a pricing policy based on the procrastination mechanism. Common to all these examples, lower costs in the present are much more attractive than promises of future discounts.

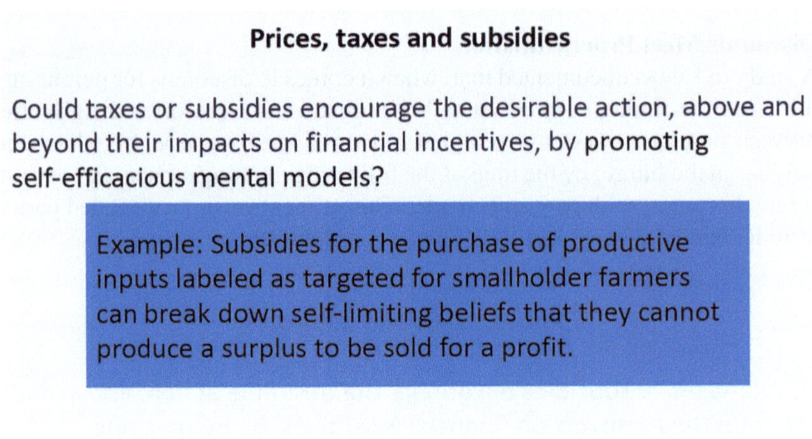

Fig. 7.12 Pricing policies vs. limiting mental models. (Source: elaborated by the authors)

In all cases, changing the timing of payments – moving them from the present to future, or vice versa – is key to address intertemporal inconsistencies. Postponing expenditures until the future or anticipating discounts to the present makes costs appear lower, decreasing the chance that desirable behaviors will be subject to procrastination in face of excessive optimism about one's future willingness to bear these costs – which is at the heart of intertemporal inconsistencies.

Limiting Mental Models

Prices, taxes, and subsidies can also activate alternative mental models and, as such, promote desirable behaviors – as long as framed effectively. Concretely, back to the previous example, framing a new subsidy for farming inputs as if it were designed specifically for smallholder farmers might activate a growth mindset (see Fig. 7.12). This is because the existence of subsidies suggests that smallholder farmers could, with investment and effort, obtain a surplus and ultimately access markets. If more farmers behaved according to this mental model after the subsidy was announced, then investments would increase far beyond what one would expect solely based on their effects on financial costs and benefits.

7.4.2 *Regulatory Policies*

Impulsivity

Regulatory policies are the most powerful tools for dealing with self-control problems. Nothing is more appropriate than prohibiting a behavior to limit the consequences of impulsivity.

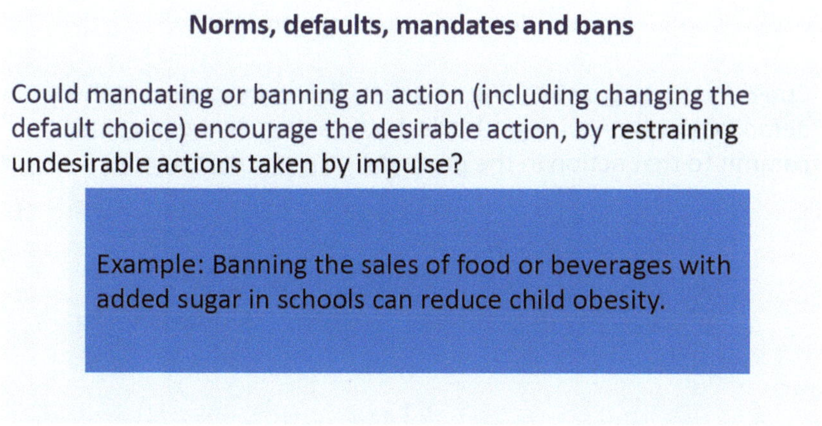

Fig. 7.13 Regulatory policies vs. impulsivity. (Source: elaborated by the authors)

Consider the problem of childhood obesity, which is associated with significant public costs worldwide. Studies suggest that the wide availability of foods with added sugar in schools is one of the main villains of this problem, in view of its addictive properties. As such, banning the sale of these products in schools could be extremely effective for addressing the impulsive behavior associated with this public problem (see Fig. 7.13).

Procrastination

As with impulsivity, mandating or banning behavior is the most direct way to address intertemporal inconsistencies. That said, these are not always feasible public policy options. For instance, it may be impractical to force a farmer to invest more resources in his or her production, or a family to invest more resources in their child's education.

Fortunately, in some of these cases, setting default options strategically can be an effective alternative to promoting desirable behaviors subject to intertemporal inconsistencies. As before, changing the choice architecture takes advantage of cognitive biases, only in this case to change the timing of costs – moving them from present into the future. Concretely, consider a program called "Save More Tomorrow",[2] which asks workers to *choose now* whether they want to increase their pension contributions as a share of their salary *by the time they get a new raise*. When this option exists, the costs of foregoing consumption to save more are only in the future.

As long as decisions cannot be easily reversed when the future finally becomes present, shifting the timing of decisions to avoid present bias tends to be effective in promoting desirable behaviors.

[2] Read more on: http://www.shlomobenartzi.com/save-more-tomorrow

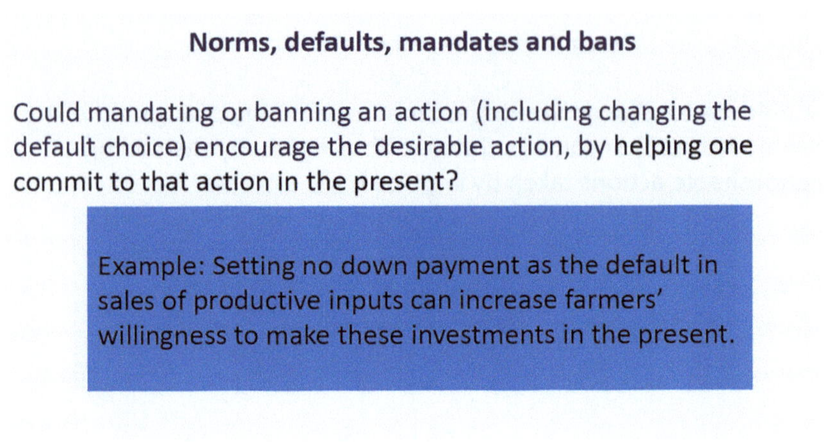

Fig. 7.14 Regulatory policies vs. procrastination. (Source: elaborated by the authors)

Back to the example of investments by smallholder farmers, removing down payments from the purchase of inputs (whenever they are paid in installments, which is common in low- and middle-income countries) shifts its costs into the future – the same horizon as the returns on investment pay out (see Fig. 7.14). It is no wonder that the absence of down payments is such a prevalent feature of retail marketing campaigns, even if consumers end up paying more overall in the absence of payments at the time of the purchase.

By the same token, as discussed earlier, making early re-enrollment in school the new standard could be an effective tool to reduce the risk of dropouts when parents procrastinate.

Limiting Mental Models

Regulatory policies can also affect limiting mental models, as long as the policy announcement induces "real citizens" to infer something about what they could achieve through their own effort.

In low- and middle-income countries, most smallholder farmers do not access markets. At most, some of them sell directly to the government, for example, to supply local public school with inputs for students' meals. If lack of access to markets is at least partly driven by limiting mental models, then regulatory policies could potentially alleviate this problem – perhaps in surprising ways. For instance, if extension workers, rural credit officers, or rural development programs mandated smallholder farmers to hand in a marketing plan as a precondition to accessing those services, then at least some of them might become convinced that it is possible to market their production – even if that would requires greater investments (see Fig. 7.15).

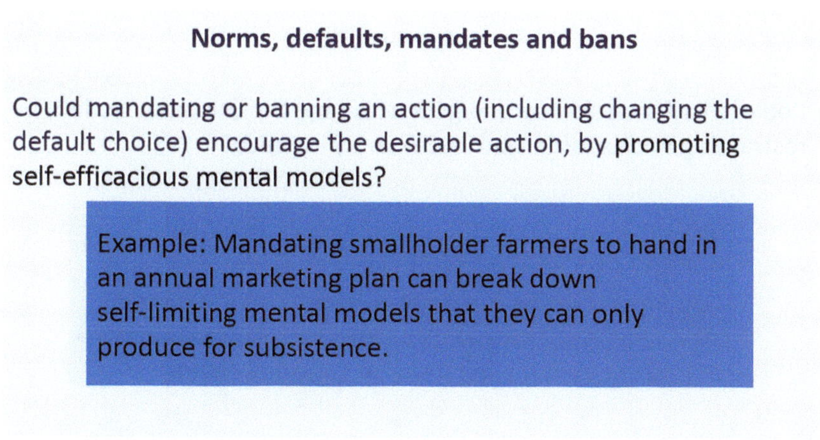

Fig. 7.15 Regulatory policies vs. limiting mental models. (Source: elaborated by the authors)

7.4.3 Information Policies

Impulsivity

Information campaigns tend not to be very promising for dealing with self-control problems in general (and impulsivity problems in particular). The reason is that information targets how individuals make plans, and the definition of impulsive behaviors is that it defies plans.

The exception to this rule is if the campaign is effective in inducing the adoption of strategies that protect the "real citizen" from impulsive behavior. In the case of childhood obesity, if the campaign is effective in inducing parents not to buy products with added sugar, or else to fill their children's lunch boxes with only healthy products (instead of sending them to school with money for snacks), then there will be little room for impulsive behavior to subvert original plans (see Fig. 7.16).

Procrastination

Information campaigns also tend to be ineffective in dealing with problems of intertemporal inconsistencies. Again, the exception is if the campaign is effective in encouraging the adoption of commitment devices that prevent the "real citizen" from deviating from his or her original plans.

Back to the example of investments by the smallholder farmers, a campaign that is effective at promoting illiquid savings might partly address the consequences of present bias by increasing the total resource pool available in the future (see Fig. 7.17). As such, even if individuals still reallocate from the future towards the present, relative to past plans, larger illiquid savings might help make up for part of these future losses.

Similarly, an effective campaign to promote savings on behalf of one's child (e.g., mobilizing resources that can only be accessed by the child herself once she

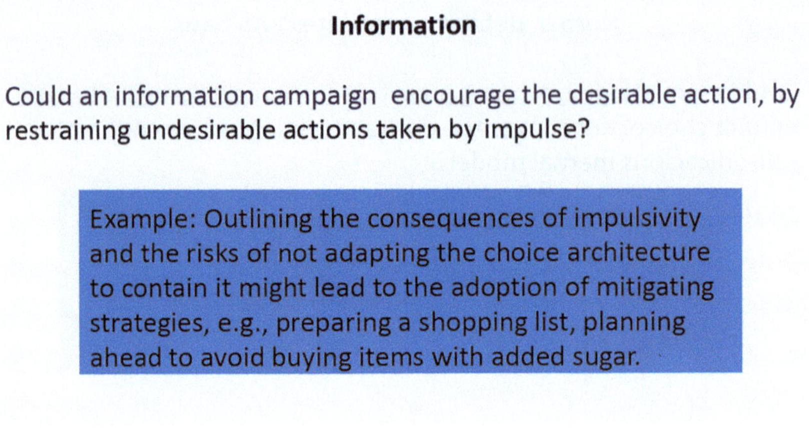

Fig. 7.16 Information policies vs. impulsivity. (Source: elaborated by the authors)

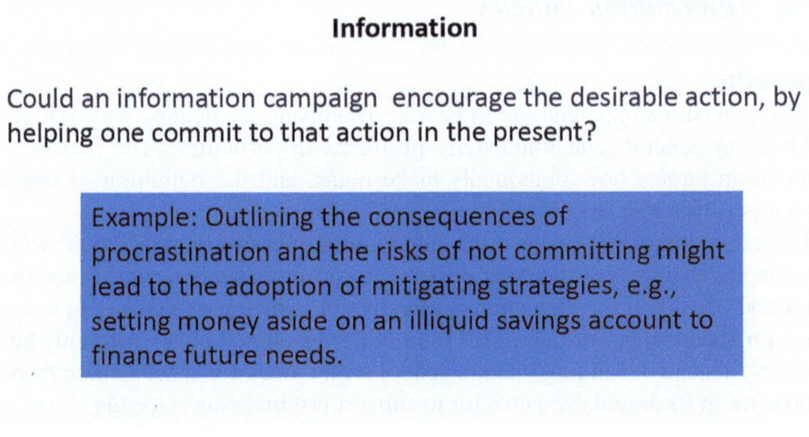

Fig. 7.17 Information policies vs. procrastination. (Source: elaborated by the authors)

turns 18) might help cover at least some of the costs of higher education, even if parents reallocate other savings in principle tagged to the children's future towards themselves as that future becomes closer. As such, illiquid savings earmarked to the child in the future can partly make up for the consequences of parent bias.

Nevertheless, it is notably difficult to encourage low- and middle-income families to save in illiquid assets. All in all, while information campaigns could in principle help mitigate the consequences of intertemporal inconsistencies, their potential to address this behavioral mechanism is most likely limited.

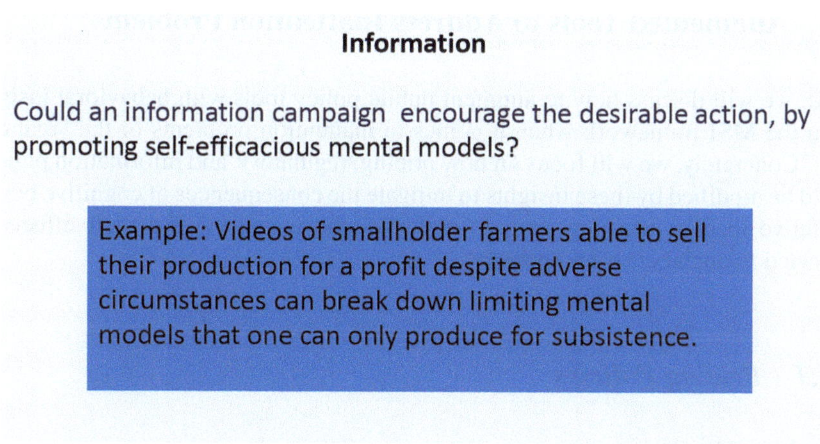

Fig. 7.18 Information policies vs. limiting mental models. (Source: elaborated by the authors)

Limiting Mental Models

In turn, information campaigns are more likely to find success when it comes to influencing mental models. Several studies illustrate effective strategies for doing so, in particular when it comes to promoting a growth mindset among teenage students. The message that the brain is "like a muscle," that is, it gets "stronger" when challenged and exercised, tends to convince at least some students that it is possible to improve relative to oneself as a result of effort – increasing their math test scores as a results. Interestingly, students targeted with growth mindset messages also tend to choose more challenging courses, presumably because they are no longer afraid of failing in these courses. After all, under a growth mindset, a good academic standing results from effort, not talent; hence, struggling is not indicative of the lack thereof.

A study in Brazil suggests that if approximately half of secondary public school students have fixed mindsets when it comes to math, simple but recurring communication via text messages (SMS) over the course of the school year can convert mindsets and improve performance in math and Portuguese tests.

Another well-established approach to promoting desirable mental models are campaigns focused on promoting role models. Successful stories from individuals with a similar background to the target audience can inspire change and promote desirable behavior. Concretely, a study in Madagascar showed that testimonials of successful former students increased student effort and their academic standing.

Back to our example of smallholder farmers, video testimonials of similar farmers sharing success stories around reinvesting profits into the future harvest could break down limiting mental models (that smallholder farmers can only produce enough for subsistence), increasing investments in production and, ultimately, unlocking access to markets (see Fig. 7.18).

7.5 Augmented Tools to Address Inattention Problems

Next, we will discuss how to augment public policy tools with behavioral insights from the MSI framework when it comes to inattention problems of the "real citizen." Concretely, we will focus on how pricing, regulatory, and information policies could be modified by these insights to mitigate the consequences of cognitive biases, cognitive load or learning through noticing, above and beyond their effects on expected financial costs and benefits.

7.5.1 Pricing Policies

Cognitive Biases

Price changes can be a powerful policy tool to reallocate real citizens'attention. Supermarkets use insights from behavioral sciences all the time to manipulate consumers' attention like no other. Discounted products are given enormous prominence on the shelf (by combining textual elements and colors), while products whose prices have gone up tend to be positioned outside the typical consumer eye level. Public managers should also take advantage of these insights, framing price changes strategically so as to reallocate attention to desirable behaviors.

Numerous studies show that those who live in poverty tend to spend much more on emergency health care than on preventive health care – even though the former could be largely avoided by investments in the latter, in particular by taking up health insurance. If this is partly driven by inattention to the future financial benefits of insurance uptake (a cognitive bias), and if subsidizing insurance successfully reallocates attention to its benefits for at least part of its target population, then take-up might increase far beyond what we would expect solely based on the effects of the subsidy on its financial costs. In effect, demand for preventive health care might increase more broadly as a result of its benefits becoming more salient – even for products that were not subsidized (see Fig. 7.19).

Cognitive Load

Subsidies are the natural policy instrument to alleviate cognitive load. After all, scarcity is what captures part of mental bandwidth needed for the brain's executive functions – including attention, memory, and impulse control – among the poor.

When mistakes driven by cognitive load are an important mechanism behind undesirable behaviors, by freeing up cognitive resources, subsidies might decrease the prevalence of these behaviors far beyond what we would expect solely based on their effects on financial incentives.

The challenge is that freeing up mental bandwidth through product-specific subsidies might require not only really large discounts, but also that these discounts are concentrated on products that amount for a significantly large fraction of the individual's total spending. Otherwise, such subsidies are likely insufficient to alleviate cognitive load.

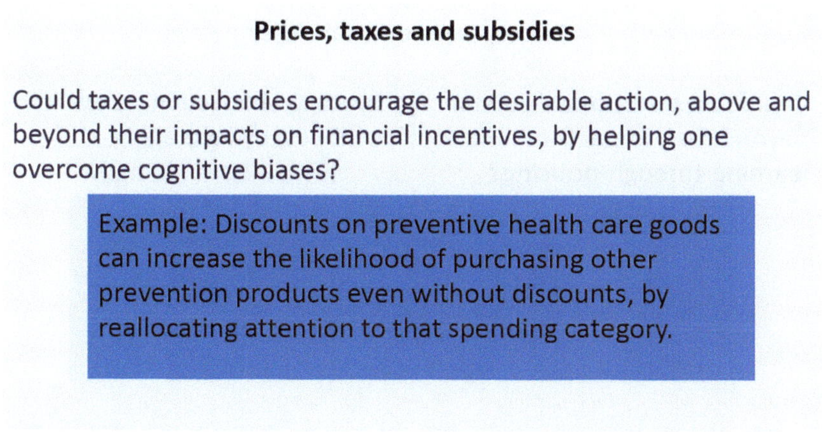

Fig. 7.19 Pricing policies vs. cognitive biases. (Source: elaborated by the authors)

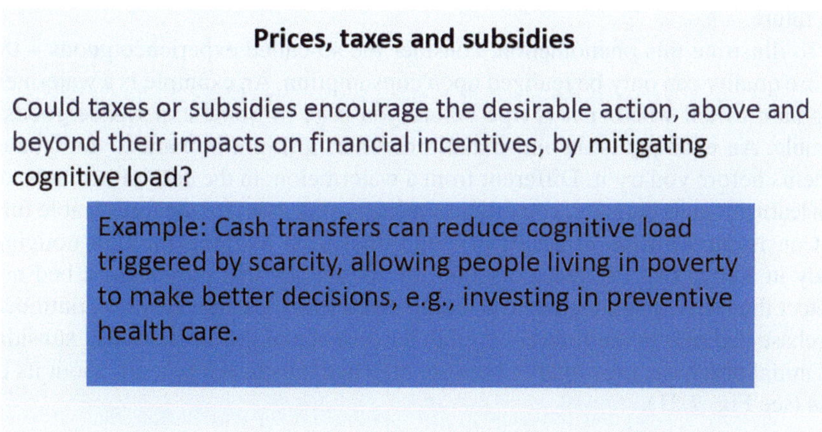

Fig. 7.20 Pricing policies vs. cognitive load. (Source: elaborated by the authors)

Cash transfers, in turn, are likely more promising. In the example of low take-up of preventive health, if this is at least partly driven by mistakes induced by cognitive load, a cash transfer program might increase take-up far beyond what we would expect solely based on their income effects (by relaxing beneficiaries' budget constraints) (see Fig. 7.20).

Learning Through Noticing

Prices, taxes, and subsidies can also influence learning through noticing. By the same logic of attention reallocation (which justifies the potential use of these policies to mitigate cognitive biases), discounts might lead "real citizens" to learn about

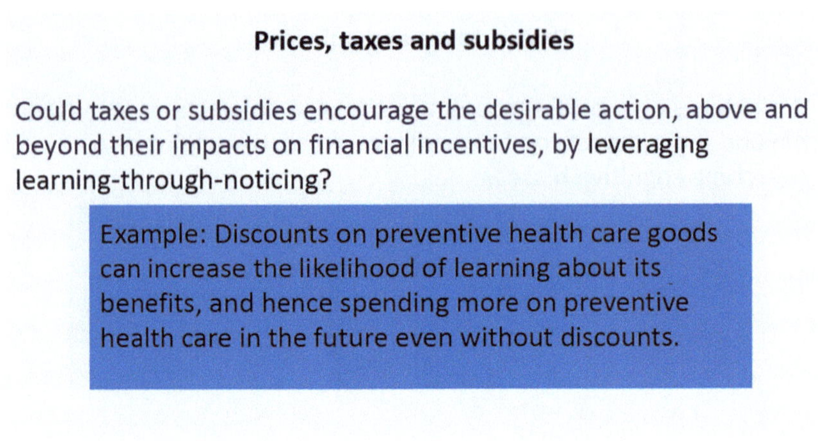

Fig. 7.21 Pricing policies vs. learning through noticing. (Source: elaborated by the authors)

the benefits of desirable decisions or behaviors – inducing them to maintain them in the future.

To illustrate this phenomenon, consider the so-called experience goods – those whose quality can only be realized upon consumption. An example is a watermelon: it is hard to tell whether it is ripe before you taste it. Some experience goods are durable. An example is an anti-malaria bed net: it might be hard to anticipate its benefits before you try it. Different from a watermelon, in the case of bed nets, once you learn about its benefits, you might continue using them for the foreseeable future.

Consistent with the effect of pricing policies on learning through noticing, a study in Kenya that offered a discount to households that purchased a bed net to protect themselves against malaria documented that these households continued to purchase bed nets in the future – even in the absence of the discount that subsidized the initial purchase, presumably because they had the chance to learn about its benefits (see Fig. 7.21).

7.5.2 Regulatory Policies

Cognitive Biases

Cognitive biases are one of the behavioral mechanisms most commonly targeted by nudges. While that might suggest that regulatory policies that fall into this category, such as setting new defaults to take advantage of status quo bias, are particularly effective, the reality of it is disappointing, in line with our discussion in previous chapters.

The case of pension contributions illustrates the limitations of regulatory policies particularly well. A study in the USA shows that setting a higher pension contribution as the default option on the HR admission form tends to substantially increase

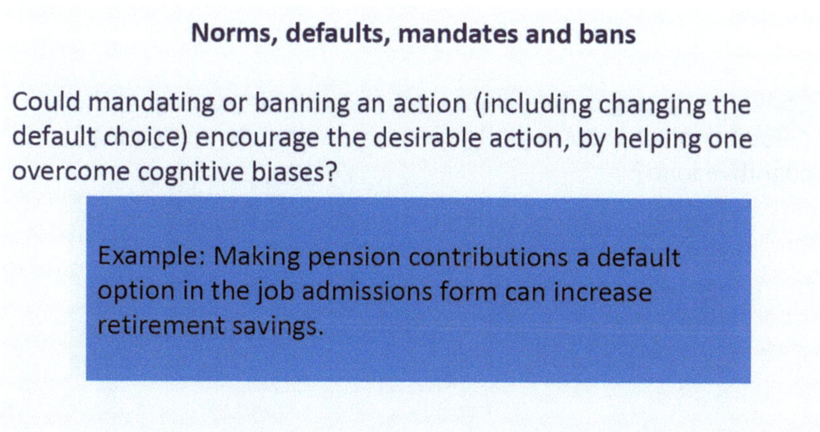

Fig. 7.22 Regulatory policies vs. cognitive biases. (Source: elaborated by the authors)

adherence to this contribution rate at first (see Fig. 7.22). Recent studies show, however, that workers tend to "undo" this positive effect when they change firms or even when they change their contract within the same firm. All in all, the net effects of such regulatory policy tend to be much more modest, in line with what the meta-analysis on the impacts of nudge units discusses for other changes to the choice architecture.

Cognitive Load

Banning undesirable behaviors or mandating desirable ones can be extremely effective in mitigating cognitive load (see Fig. 7.23). The reason is simple: in the absence of choice, there is no scope for mistakes.

In *Poor Economics*, Abhijit Banerjee and Esther Duflo (both winners of the 2019 Nobel Prize in Economics) point out that people in poverty typically have to make a much larger number of decisions than the rich. In a typical sub-Saharan African country, to ensure that her children drink clean water, a mother needs to fetch water from a clean source, ensure that it will be carried in a bucket that is also clean, add chlorine to ensure that water might not become infected on the way or at home, and still boil the water to ensure that it is ultimately safe to consume. There are many possibilities for decision errors – in particular, those driven by cognitive load – at each step of this long decision chain. In contrast, in wealthy countries, it is enough to merely open the tap. Offering everyone clean water without requiring them to make the right choices is a regulatory policy.

In the example of pension contributions, making them mandatory would naturally protect the "real citizen" from their own biases. Mandatory contributions assure a high enough income stream to live off during retirement, without requiring the "real citizen" to actively decide how much he or she should save – which typically involves complex calculations, the more so for those who are under cognitive load.

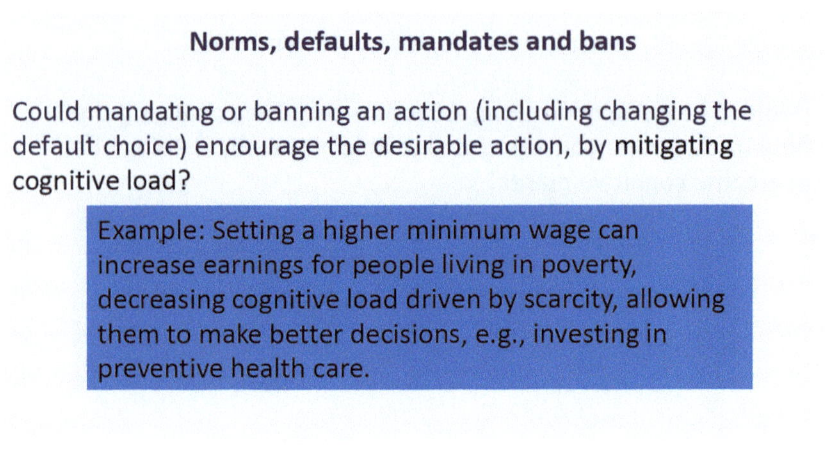

Fig. 7.23 Regulatory policies vs. cognitive load. (Source: elaborated by the authors)

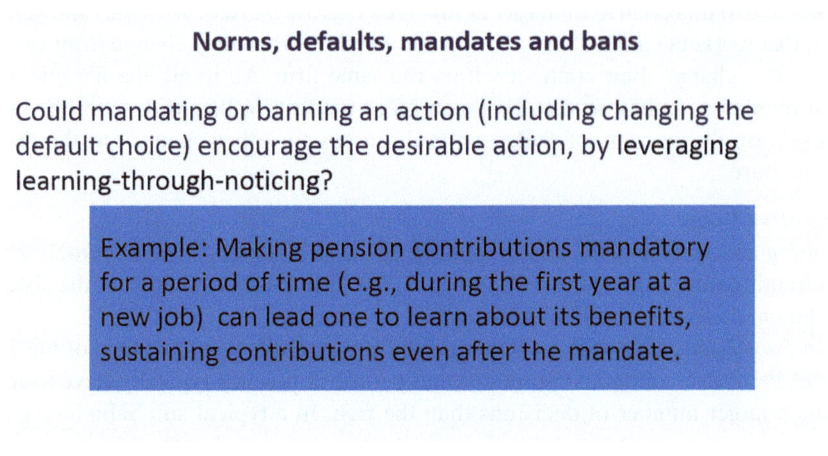

Fig. 7.24 Regulatory policies vs. learning through noticing. (Source: elaborated by the authors)

Learning Through Noticing

As with pricing policies, regulation can also influence learning through noticing by reallocating attention to the benefits of certain desirable decisions or behaviors, which might then likely be maintained in the future.

Back to the example of pension contributions, making high rates compulsory for a limited period of time might end up inducing citizens to keep them afterwards – even after the mandate is long gone – as long as "real citizens" learn about the benefits of saving more for retirement during the mandate (see Fig. 7.24).

7.5.3 *Information Policies*

Cognitive Biases

Information campaigns can be powerful instruments to reallocate real citizens' attention, far beyond their informational content. Their success might depend on effectively leveraging communication features – from the frequency of communication to interactivity to how messages are framed – so as to make the decision domain that they target more salient.

Information Campaigns Meet Cognitive Biases

A study in Brazil illustrates that logic through an experiment. Researchers found that parents of secondary school students tend to underestimate how often their children miss classes. Sending these parents weekly information about their children's truancies (via text messages) increased student attendance and ultimately improved learning outcomes (see Fig. 7.25).

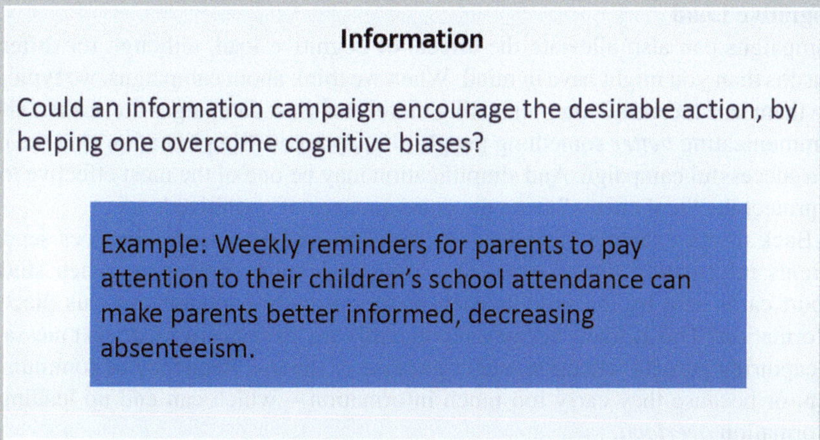

Fig. 7.25 Information policies vs. cognitive biases. (Source: elaborated by the authors)

While one might think that results were driven by messages making parents more accurate directly, an alternative intervention – which only tried to increase the salience of children's school life, encouraging parents to follow it more closely, but not conveying information specific to the circumstance of the recipient – had exactly the same effects.

If anything, such uninformative nudges worked even better than information, because they affected behavior across all subjects (while information improved outcomes only within the subjects it provided information on) and the more so among those who were targeted by more frequent communication.

Read more:

Lichand, Guilherme, Eric Bettinger, Nina Cunha e Ricardo Madeira (2022), When the Effects of Educational Interventions Are Driven by Salience – Evidence from School Parents in Brazil. https://papers.ssrn.com/sol3/papers.cfm?abstract_id=3644124].

How can it be that information and nudges had similar effects if only the former made parents more accurate in that study? The researchers documented that the reason was that both interventions led parents to collect decision-relevant information themselves: while no intervention ever communicated student report card grades, in both cases parents became more accurate relative to those who did not receive messages from the school. These results are consistent with the claim that both campaigns made children's school life more salient.

Cognitive Load

Campaigns can also alleviate the effects of cognitive load, although for different reasons than you might have in mind. When we think about campaigns, we typically see them as a means of communicating more. But most campaigns are, rather, about communicating *better* something people already know. Simplification is at the root of a successful campaign. And simplification may be one of the most effective tools to protect the "real citizen" from the consequences of cognitive load.

Back to our example of nudges in education just discussed, why does sending parents information via text message improve learning outcomes, when student report cards sent by the schools each quarter already communicate this piece of information? This is likely because report cards are less effective than text messages in capturing parents' attention, either because of the low frequency of communication, or because they carry too much information – which can end up leading to information *overload*.

In such a context, simplification can produce powerful results. A recent study shows that simplifying court summons forms to highlight the hearing date and the consequences of nonattendance dramatically reduced incarceration for that reason in the USA. In the previous example, this logic suggests that simplifying the way report cards are presented could improve educational outcomes even without (or beyond) recurring nudges (see Fig. 7.26).

Because of the regressive incidence of cognitive load, simplification is not only effective, but also, essentially progressive.

Learning Through Noticing

Last, information campaigns can also be effective instruments against learning through noticing. While campaigns can reallocate attention to desirable behaviors in one-off decisions, they can also induce permanent behavior change – by increasing the salience of the benefits of desirable behaviors, which might have been previously overlooked by the "real citizen."

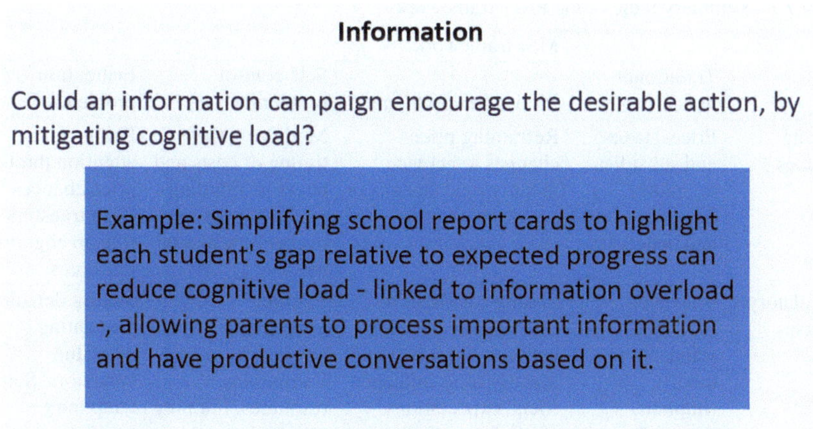

Fig. 7.26 Information policies vs. cognitive load. (Source: elaborated by the authors)

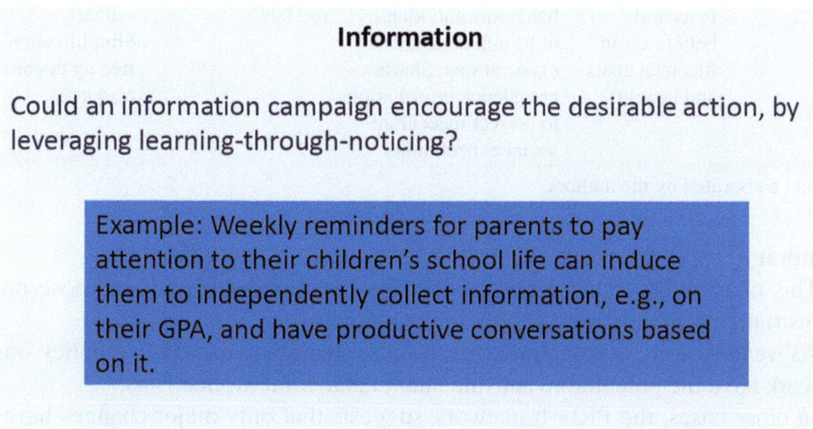

Fig. 7.27 Information policies vs. learning through noticing. (Source: elaborated by the authors)

Back to our nudges in the education example, the study shows that weekly text messages led parents to collect information on their own (see Fig. 7.27). As a result, they became more accurate about their children's GPA even though no text message had ever conveyed them as part of either campaign. Both campaigns presumably triggered learning through noticing: a permanent increase in the extent to which parents' monitored their children's school life, with impacts on their attendance and grades – and, perhaps most importantly, on their self-esteem and future aspirations.

Table 7.1 presents a summary of the PRIx framework, along with examples of traditional uses and promising behaviorally-augmented policies in each case.

Table 7.1 Summary table of the PRIx framework

	Traditional uses	MSI framework Motivation problems	Self-control problems	Inattention problems
Pricing policies	Prices, taxes, and subsidies to modify financial costs and benefits.	Reframing price changes to activate identity mechanisms or social pressure.	Modifying the timing of costs and benefits. Framing price changes to trigger new mental models.	Reallocating attention through price changes. Cash transfers to free up cognitive resources.
Regulatory policies	Mandates, bans, and standards to modify (implicit) financial costs and benefits.	Setting standards to modify associations between behaviors and identity or to influence social expectations. Changing visibility to turn up or down social pressure.	Banning undesirable behaviors. Earmarking resources. Framing standards to trigger new mental models.	Setting defaults. Mandating desirable behaviors. Setting temporary mandates to unlock learning through noticing.
Information policies	Campaigns to correct inaccurate beliefs about financial costs and benefits.	Campaigns to modify associations between behaviors and identity or to influence social expectations. Sharing prevalence information to correct inaccurate social expectations.	Campaigns to change mental models.	Making financial costs and benefits salient. Simplification to free up cognitive resources.

Source: elaborated by the authors

Summary
1. This chapter presented a framework for public managers to repurpose policy instruments already used widely in the public sector.
2. As we have seen, in some cases, even small changes to the existing policy framework have the potential to activate latent behavioral mechanisms.
3. In other cases, the PRIx framework suggests that only major changes have the potential to successfully overcome behavioral constraints that affect the real citizen. As the chapter emphasized, not all policy tools hold promise for successfully addressing the behavioral mechanisms that condition how real citizens make choices. Effective policies, hence, depend on identifying the most plausible behavioral mechanisms at play and the most feasible policies to address them - a roadmap that we turn to in the following chapters.

Suggested Readings

Gneezy, Uri and Rustichini, Aldo "A Fine is a Price", Journal of Legal Studies, vol. 29, n. 1, january. 2000. Available at SSRN: https://ssrn.com/abstract=180117

Alcott, Hunt, Social Norms and Energy Conservation. Journal of Public Economics, Vol. 95, No 9-10, October 2011, pages 1082-1095.

DUFLO, Esther, KREMER, Michael, and ROBINSON, Jonathan (2011a) "Nudging Farmers to Use Fertilizer: Theory and Experimental Evidence from Kenya", The American Economic Review, vol. 101(6), pp. 2350-90, october. 2011.

BURSZTYN, Leonardo, FUJIWARA, Thomas, and PALLAIS, Amanda (2017) "'Acting Wife': Marriage Market Incentives and Labor Market Investments", The American Economic Review, v. 107, n.11, pp. 3288-3319, november. 2017.

BURSZTYN, Leonardo, GONZALES Alessandra, and YANAGIZAWA-DROTT, David (2020) "Misperceived Social Norms: Female Labor Force Participation in Saudi Arabia", The American Economic Review, v. 110 (10), pp. 2997-3029. 2020.

Bursztyn, Leonard, e Robert Jensen, How Does Peer Pressure Affect Educational Investments? The Quarterly Journal of Economics, Volume 130, Issue 3, August 2015, Pages 1329–1367.

DUFLO, Esther, Michael KREMER, and Jonathan ROBINSON (2011b) "Nudging Farmers to Use Fertilizer: Theory and Experimental Evidence from Kenya", The American Economic Review, 101(6), pp. 2350-90.

CASABURI, Lorenzo, e Jack WILLIS (2018) "Time Vs. State Insurance: Experimental Evidence From Contract Farming in Kenya", The American Economic Review, 108(2), pp. 3778-3813.

ROBERTO, Christina A. How psychological insights can inform food policies to address unhealthy eating habits. American Psychologist, v. 75, n. 2, p. 265, 2020.

Thaler, Richard & Benartzi, Shlomo. (2007). Heuristics and Biases in Retirement Savings Behavior. Journal of Economic Perspectives. vol. 21. n. 3, pp. 81-104, august. 2007. Available at: https://doi.org/10.1257/jep.21.3.81

DWECK, C. S. (2006). Mindset: the new psychology of success. New York, Random House.

CLARO, Susana, David PAUNESKU, and Carol S. Dweck (2016) "Growth Mindset Tempers the Effects of Poverty on Academic Achievement." PNAS, 113(31), pp. 8664-8668.

JOB, Veronika, Carol S. DWECK, and Gregory WALTON (2010) "Ego Depletion - Is It All In Your Head? Implicit Theories About Willpower Affect Self-Regulation," Psychological Science, 21(11), pp. 1686-93.

XXX, (n.d.)

YEAGER, David S. et al (2019) "A National Experiment Reveals Where a Growth Mindset Improves Achievement", Nature, vol. 573, pp. 364–369, august. 2019.

LICHAND, Guilherme et al. The impacts of remote learning in secondary education during the pandemic in Brazil. Nature Human Behaviour, p. 1-8, 2022a.

LICHAND, Guilherme et al. Association of COVID-19 incidence and mortality rates with school reopening in Brazil during the COVID-19 pandemic. In: JAMA Health Forum. American Medical Association, 2022b. p. e215032.

LICHAND, Guilherme, WOLF, Sharon. Measuring Child Labor: Whom Should Be Asked, and Why It Matters. Available at SSRN, 2022.

Cohen, Jessica, and Pascaline, Dupas (2010) "Free Distribution or Cost-Sharing? Evidence from a Randomized Malaria Prevention Experiment, The Quarterly Journal of Economics, vol. 125, Issue 1, pp. 1–45, february. 2010. Available at: https://doi.org/10.1162/qjec.2010.125.1.1

DELLAVIGNA, Stefano, and Elizabeth LINOS (2020) "RCTs to Scale: Comprehensive Evidence from Two Nudge Units," NBER Working Paper, n. 27594, july. 2020.

MADRIAN, Brigitte C.; SHEA, Dennis F. The power of suggestion: Inertia in 401 (k) participation and savings behavior. The Quarterly journal of economics, v. 116, n. 4, p. 1149-1187, 2001.

Arnoud, A., Choukhmane, T., Colmenares, J., O'Dea, C., & Parvathaneni, A. (2021). The Evolution of US Firms' Retirement Plan O erings: Evidence from a New Panel Data Set1.

Lichand, Guilherme, Eric Bettinger, Nina Cunha e Ricardo Madeira (2022), When the Effects of Educational Interventions Are Driven by Salience – Evidence from School Parents in Brazil. https://papers.ssrn.com/sol3/papers.cfm?abstract_id=3644124]

Chapter 8
Using Behavioral Insights in Practice

8.1 Introduction

The previous chapters discussed extensively the behavioral mechanisms that affect how "real citizens" make plans, and their ability to follow through on those plans. We also discussed at length how pricing, regulatory, and information policies can be augmented by these behavioral insights, accounting for real citizens' motivation, self-control, and inattention problems with the goal of more effectively mitigating externalities and social inequalities.

In theory, we now know what to do. In practice, however, where do we start? Where should you, reader, begin your journey to apply what you have learned to the social problems you have to address?

This chapter provides strategies for identifying the structural and behavioral mechanisms most likely relevant for the problem at hand, drawing from systems thinking and cognitive psychology techniques. Such tentative mechanisms can then be used to inform policy prototypes, which can keep evolving in terms of fidelity and complexity as the hypotheses behind them are progressively validated.

As it will become clear, this process is meant to be iterative. It is all about formulating hypotheses informed by the system (as discussed in the previous chapters), and then testing these hypotheses to learn about which mechanisms seem most relevant to the audience who will be targeted by the policy. Testing hypotheses involves scientific methods, but there is also some art to the craft – we share best practices and common mistakes in the following chapter.

In this chapter, we illustrate how this process works in practice with the help of a leading example: the problem of low demand for preventive health care.

G. Lichand et al., *Behavioral Insights for Policy Design*,
https://doi.org/10.1007/978-3-031-33034-6_8

8.2 Screening Structural and Behavioral Mechanisms

The first step for identifying relevant structural and behavioral mechanisms is to spend time understanding the problem in depth. Informed by this understanding, one can start by guessing which mechanisms are unlikely to play a relevant role in the problem at hand, even before testing them in practice. Screening based on what we already know about the problem is key; after all, rigorous testing takes scarce financial and time resources, which requires us to focus on a few promising hypotheses. In the following, we discuss strategies to screen such promising structural and behavioral mechanisms.

8.2.1 Start with the (sub) System

The starting point for identifying promising structural and behavioral mechanisms for a social problem is to ensure that the problem is properly mapped, especially when it comes to its potential systemic effects. This is because the behavioral mechanisms with the most critical public repercussions are the ones that reinforce vicious cycles. Identifying these mechanisms can shed light on which policy tools might be capable of breaking the cycles or, better yet, of generating virtuous cycles. The previous chapters discuss this systemic approach in detail, covering the concepts and tools to map systemic forces in an accessible way.

With these tools, a practical way to start is by mapping subsystems. We illustrate that approach for our problem of low demand for preventive health care. The subsystem illustrates a cycle in which low demand for preventive health care implies low use of these products and services, which in turn implies that children growing up in this context are likely to be affected by conditions that, while easily preventable, will end up jeopardizing their future opportunities – either directly, because of the consequences of these diseases on child development, or indirectly, because of the school days lost or learning impaired by these conditions. It is important to mention that this problem is, of course, embedded in a larger system, which includes the forces that keep families living in poverty in this condition.

The vicious cycle mapped in this subsystem could be turned into a virtuous cycle: a policy that increased demand for preventive health care would tend to increase the usage of preventive products, likely with positive consequences for children's health, their educational outcomes, and their future trajectories (see Fig. 8.1).

Parents' beliefs about the connection between preventive health spending in the present and children's future employment and income prospects are a key factor in their decisions of how much to spend on prevention. If parents think that a child has a low future potential, they will invest little in him or her across all dimensions, including preventive health care.

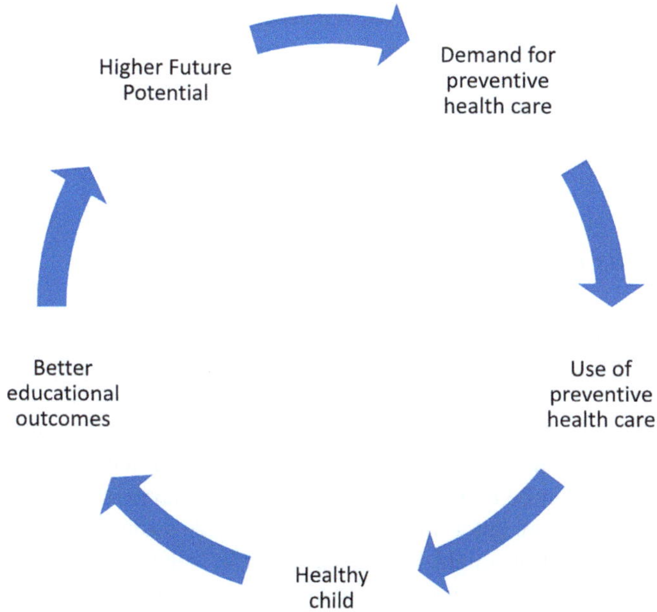

Fig. 8.1 Mapping subsystems. (Source: elaborated by the authors)

This subsystem illustrates various opportunities for policy intervention at different points in the cycle. The simplest way to formulate hypotheses is to ask why, at one point in the cycle, an intervention might fail to break a vicious cycle (or to promote a virtuous one) at the immediate next step. For instance, is it possible that, if families were provided preventive health care for free, its uptake might still be low? This could be explained by hypotheses leveraging different mechanisms. Some are structural (i.e., those that would affect even the "ideal citizen"), like the need to work double shifts and weekends, which might prevent those living in poverty from waiting long hours to access free preventive health care; others, behavioral.

Other examples: Could it be the case that, even if families did use preventive health care services, their children would still be unhealthy? Or, even if they become healthy, that their performance in school would not improve? Or, even if their academic standing improves, that they remain unprepared to successfully enter the labor market in the future? Each of those could be explained through different hypotheses, possibly leveraging completely different structural and behavioral mechanisms.

As such, carefully identifying the different hypotheses that could help explain why the social problem at hand tends to persist in the context of the (sub) system is a precondition for moving on to the next steps of the behavioral diagnostics.

Should one exhaust all possible hypotheses that might explain why a social problem might resist policy interventions? This seems like a daunting task. Fortunately, here systems thinking can help us make progress. As the previous chapter discusses, leverage points offer a good starting point for formulating hypotheses. By restricting attention to leverage points, at least at first, one can analyze the structural and behavioral mechanisms relevant for systemic levers, precisely where interventions have the highest potential to transform the system.

Once the relevant hypotheses have been identified, how to identify which of them seem more or less plausible? This is what we will discuss next.

8.2.2 Focus on a Hypothesis

As much as every public problem is possibly related to many different hypotheses, our previous discussion suggests that it is important to address only one hypothesis at a time.

Back to our example of low demand for preventive health, the hypothesis that households may not use preventive health products or services even when they are available for free can be explained by structural or behavioral mechanisms. Using the MSI framework, the latter might include inaccurate social expectations, if families fear that prevention might be looked down by others; procrastination in the decision to bring the family to the health clinic; or cognitive biases associated with inattention to the benefits of prevention uptake.

In turn, the hypothesis that, even as children's health improves as a result of higher uptake of preventive health care, their labor market prospects may not improve, could be explained by structural mechanisms (e.g., beliefs that education contributes little to acquiring skills relevant to future earnings) or by behavioral mechanisms. Using the MSI framework, the latter might include parent bias, whereby parents systematically reallocate resources initially set to children towards themselves; or learning through noticing, whereby parents systematically ignore their children's school effort.

These two examples highlight that each hypothesis deals with different social problems, possibly associated with completely different mechanisms. For this reason, behavioral diagnostics needs to address one problem at a time. Choose one hypothesis to start with and move on to the next one only when the diagnosis is complete.

8.2.3 Discard Implausible Mechanisms and Unfeasible Policies

Once the working hypothesis has been set, the next step is to define which mechanisms will be subject to testing.

Our previous discussion illustrates that, even when focusing on a single hypothesis, with enough creativity, the number of potential structural and behavioral mechanisms that affect the problem in question can still be very large. This requires eliminating some mechanisms; not because they are not conceptually possible, but because they may be less *plausible* than others in the context of the problem at hand, or because they may motivate policies that *are not feasible* in this context.

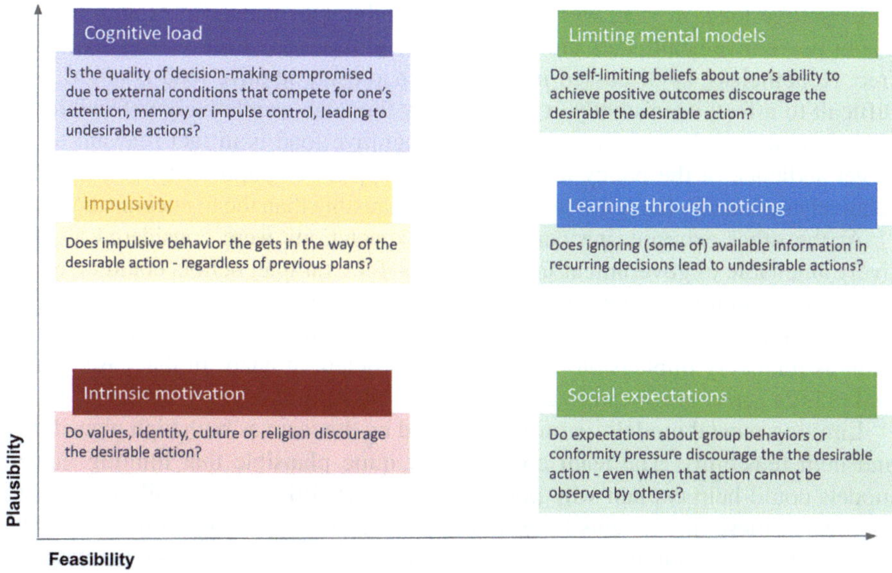

Fig. 8.2 Feasibility vs. plausibility matrix. (Source: elaborated by the authors)

Back to our preventive health care example, the hypothesis of low usage even when prevention is available for free could be explained by numerous behavioral mechanisms. Fig. 8.2 tries to categorize some of them according to the principles of plausibility (on the vertical axis) and feasibility (on the horizontal axis) just discussed, using inputs from a team of Brazilian public managers – all tenured public servants working at the federal behavioral insights team (GNova), with whom we conducted this conceptual classification exercise in 2021.

The further to the left of the graph, the smaller the possibility of affecting the mechanism through the policies available to government *in that context* (i.e., the less feasible it is to address it given local constraints). The further down the graph, the lower the likelihood that the mechanism is relevant *as perceived by the policy team* (i.e., the less plausible it is to the problem in question). The emphases in the previous sentences are key. Feasibility may depend on the team in which the public manager is embedded, as well as on elements outside his or her domain, including the political landscape. Just the same, plausibility is not an objective measure but, rather, reflects the prior beliefs of the team involved in the diagnosis, subject to revision if testing ultimately refutes some of these initial hypotheses.

In the figure, lack of intrinsic motivation was not only rated by the team as relatively implausible to explain the low take-up of preventive health when it is freely available but also, as relatively hard to affect, given the policy context of the team. As such, it makes little sense to allocate scarce resources to try to gauge whether this mechanism is relevant to the target audience, relative to other mechanisms that the team rated as both more plausible and amenable to policy interventions.

Cognitive load, in turn, was rated as a plausible mechanism to explain the low use of preventive health care among those living in poverty even when prevention-free. Nonetheless, as discussed in previous chapters, cognitive load is notoriously difficult to affect; consistently, it was rated by the team as relatively unfeasible. As such, it makes little sense to test whether cognitive load is in fact relevant to the target audience of the policy team. The same applies to impulsivity, also rated as relatively unfeasible (and, worse, rated as less plausible than the former mechanism).

At the other extreme, inaccurate social expectations were considered as relatively amenable to government interventions – for example, beliefs could be easily corrected by an information campaign that shares the true prevalence of prevention uptake among the target audience. Nonetheless, the mechanism was rated by the team as relatively implausible to explain the problem at hand. In that case, it also makes little sense to allocate scarce resources to testing it.

Limiting mental models, in turn, were rated by the team as both high plausibility and high feasibility. The team considered it quite plausible that limiting mental models could help explain why poor parents invest little in their children's health even when these investments have no costs. There was also consensus around the idea that limiting mental models could be addressed in a relatively simple way, for example, through a campaign highlighting as role models positive deviant parents – those who, under the same circumstances, took up free prevention services, averting health problems that would have ultimately gotten in the way of their children's futures. According to both criteria, this mechanism emerges as an excellent candidate to be tested in practice with the target audience of the policy team.

But taking a single mechanism to test can be very risky. If it turns out that the prior beliefs of the policy team were off, and this mechanism proves to be of little relevance, testing must start again from scratch – having wasted time and other valuable resources. To minimize that risk, it might be desirable to run tests as horse races: testing competing mechanisms with high feasibility, even if some of them are considered relatively less plausible at first.

In our example, learning through noticing was rated as high feasibility because the team considered it could be somewhat easily affected, for example, by weekly reminders encouraging parents to pay attention to their children's health conditions. Even if less plausible, this mechanism should be included in the testing phase. After all, thinking like a behavioral scientist requires being open to having your beliefs refuted by empirical results.

In practice, plausibility and feasibility are fluid concepts; different policy teams may disagree over how to rank different mechanisms in both criteria. Ultimately, screening which mechanisms to test first is a process prone to errors. What matters, as previously highlighted, is to be aware that this process is meant to be iterative: the team should continuously learn from their interactions with the target audience, as well as from new background information that becomes available, to update their ratings over time.

The more mechanisms with high feasibility and some plausibility that can be tested, the greater the scope for learning. Having said that, these benefits must be contrasted to the costs and constraints of experimentation – to which we will turn next.

Screening Mechanisms

Let us take the example of female labor force participation in Saudi Arabia. Assume that, in this system, the policy team identifies that the relevant leverage point is husbands' beliefs about social disapproval, motivated by the hypothesis that even if both husband and wife would privately support that she works outside of the home, husbands might still decide against it.

As in other cases, this hypothesis could be explained by a number of structural and behavioral mechanisms, so we must analyze their feasibility and plausibility to determine which hypothesis should be prioritized for testing in the next step.

Considering that leverage is related to social factors, we can easily associate it with social expectations and social image concerns. It is also possible to argue that unsupportive husbands suffer from limiting mental models (associating certain occupations with gender stereotypes) and learning through noticing (ignoring that some wives already actively participate in the labor force or failing to revisit their decisions from time to time). As such, we have up to four mechanisms that could be tested in the field.

Important remark: Do not forget to also rate structural mechanisms when it comes to their plausibility and feasibility! Even if, motivated by the MSI-PRIx framework, the policy team wants to focus on behavioral mechanisms, accounting for structural constraints might be key to designing policies that stand a real chance of changing behavior in the real world, often in combination with behavioral mechanisms.

8.3 Testing Hypotheses with Vignettes

Next, we will discuss how to test the relevance of the screened structural and behavioral mechanisms with the target audience of the policy team.

8.3.1 *What Vignettes Are and How They Work*

Understanding whether a mechanism is actually behind an undesirable behavior is extremely challenging. Imagine asking parents living in poverty "do you not use preventive health care because of limiting mental models?"

Clearly, this is not the kind of question to which one can expect very revealing answers. The central problem is not just that some of these concepts can be hard to grasp. Even if we were to strip them down to basics, making them accessible to a wide audience, such questions likely induce the so-called *social desirability biases* – the tendency not to answer truthfully but, rather, to say what one thinks the interviewer wants to hear.

When a poor parent is asked whether he or she thinks that part of the problem is that they believe that investing in their children does not pay off, he or she will likely be inclined to say "no" even when they might firmly hold this beliefs. After all, answering affirmatively would most likely be interpreted unfavorably by the interviewer.

Instead of asking them directly, we can try to use indirect elicitation techniques, drawing from cognitive psychology. One such technique is vignette experiments. Vignettes are representations describing a circumstance or scenario, representative of reality or fictional, allowing one to assess beliefs, attitudes, and/or behaviors. Vignette experiments place characters in situations similar to those experienced by the target audience, across different scenarios that vary with respect to strategic features to which the experimenter wants to elicit participants' reactions. Concretely, in a first scenario, the vignette might depict a poor family that must decide whether to take their child for preventive exams, available for free at the health center. After describing the story, the interviewer asks the participant how the parents in the story feel, what they think, and how they are likely to decide. By talking about a character with whom they identify, rather than about themselves, the interviewee tends to feel more at ease, and their answers tend to be less affected by social desirability biases.

The key to the experiment is to compare participants' answers across different scenarios. To test the relevance of limiting mental models, another scenario might describe the same situation, but supplement the description of the original scenario (or *control* version, using the language of experiments) with the story of another family who took their child for checkups and, thanks to this, managed to avoid emergency expenses or a serious condition, thus ensuring a better future for their child. This extended description can have additional visual elements, if necessary, to make the story more concrete. As in the control version, after describing the story, the interviewer asks the participant how the parents feel, what they think, and how they are likely to decide.

Comparing response patterns between the control and modified scenarios can reveal the relative importance of different mechanisms (as long as the experiment follows best practices and avoids common mistakes; see next chapter). Concretely, suppose that 30% of participants answered that the family would make the investment in the control scenario, but 75% of them answered that they would do so in the modified scenario. This significant change suggests that limiting mental models might be relevant in this context. Alternatively, if in the modified version this percentage remained around 30%, we would conclude that limiting mental models are likely not very relevant amongst the target audience in the context of this problem.

One can present different scenarios to different participants (randomly assigned), compare the answers of each participant across different scenarios (randomizing the order in which they are presented), or both.

Vignette Experiments

Back to our example of female labor force participation in Saudi Arabia, consider the three scenarios below:

A. Ahmad is married to Maryam and the two of them have been facing financial difficulties. Maryam suggests to Ahmad that she could work to help with the household bills.
B. Ahmad is married to Maryam and the two of them have been facing financial difficulties. Maryam suggests to Ahmad that she could work to help with the household bills. Later that day, the two of them watch a soap opera together, in which the main character's wife works outside the home. Maryam mentions it to her husband as an example that working wives are a reality.
C. Ahmad is married to Maryam and the two of them have been facing financial difficulties. Maryam suggests to Ahmad that she could work to help with the household bills. Talking to some friends, Ahmad finds out that they have no quibble with their wives working outside the home, but they fear that this might lead others to perceive them as a bad husband.

Each participant was only presented with one scenario, randomly assigned. After the vignette, all participants were asked two questions: "Do you think the husband in the story would support his wife if she were to look for a job outside the home?" and "From 0 to 100%, what does he think is the share of other husbands who would support their wives if they were to look for a job outside the home?"

By comparing both answers across scenarios, the policy team could gauge the plaubility of the mechanisms of interest – concretely, the extent to which the mechanism that each scenario focuses on likely affects husbands' first- and higher-order beliefs, i.e., attitudes (part of intrinsic motivations) and social expectations in the context of this problem. The experimentation process can be organized using a Vignette Canvas (see Table 8.1).

Table 8.1 Structuring vignette experiment to assess the plausibiligy of structural and behavioral mechanisms

Public Problem	Target audience	Mechanisms	Attitudes	Behaviors
Economically active women in Saudi Arabia cannot work outside the home without challenging social norms and obtaining the approval of their male "guardians."	*Audience* Male "guardians" of economically active Saudi women	Social expectations	Expects no other husband to support women working outise the home	Prevents his wife from working outside the home when other husbands' support is unkown to him
	Environment Household	Social image concerns	Worries about what others will think of him in case he supports his wife working outside the home	Prevents his wife from working outside the home in activities that are very visible to others

Source: elaborated by the authors

The canvas highlights the differences between the mechanisms that the different scenarios focus on: *social expectations* stem from inaccurate beliefs about other husbands' attitudes (and accompanying social sanctions from not conforming to group norms), whereas *social image concerns* are about the public visibility of defying such norms. Vignette experiments can help narrow down which mechanism is more plausible in the context of this problem. Naturally, if it would be unfeasible to change the visibility of female labor force participation in economic activities outside the home, then it would be natural to focus policy interventions on social expectations – to the extent that the mechanism is found to be relevant among the target audience.

Tip
Check the toolkit presented in Chap. 12.

The following chapter addresses best practices and common mistakes when it comes to testing behavioral mechanisms. Section 12.6 in Chap. 12 further includes a wireframe to help you build your own vignettes.

8.3.2 Learning About Mechanisms Versus Solutions

Back to our example of low demand for preventive health care, the scenario in the vignette experiment addressing limiting mental models seemed to test more than just the mechanism itself. That scenario described something akin to a public policy tool: its focus on role models had elements of an information campaign, embedded in the application of the vignette. As such, it is tempting to conclude that the test allows learning directly about potential solutions.

Nevertheless, this conclusion is undesirable, for at least two reasons. First, that would limit vignette design to scenarios that already include candidate solutions. This would force the policy team to skip steps (remember, we are still at the diagnostics stage!). In contrast, vignettes allow the imaginative freedom to turn mechanisms on or off directly, unattached to specific interventions, such that the team does not need to spend time thinking about potential solutions suited to the context of their target audience at this early stage.

In the example, the modified scenario could, instead, explicitly mention the family's mental model when considering the decision to uptake preventive health care. Concretely, the vignette could state that the family believes that the future of an individual and that of their child are basically sealed, and that there is not much that can be done to change them. Alternatively, the vignette could word it the other way around, stating that the family believes that they can always improve their situation by making the right decisions in situations with important consequences for their future. Comparing participants' responses in any of these scenarios to the control scenario would already be enough to reveal how relevant this mechanism might be in the context of the problem at hand.

The second reason why learning about mechanisms is not necessarily informative about the best solutions to address them is directly linked to the PRIx framework. As we have discussed in previous chapters, limiting mental models might be addressed by different policy tools, above and beyond information campaigns – pricing and regulatory policies might also potentially activate different mental models. Which policy instrument is ultimately best suited for the task depends on specific tests (such as prototyping, which we will discuss below). Vignette experiments, in turn, tend to be more conceptual, and hence more helpful for diagnosing causes than for designing solutions.

You can use the MSI-PRIx board to help you identify the behavioral mechanisms most promising for the problem at hand, along with potential policies augmented by these insights (see sample excerpt in Fig. 8.3). The material is available in the toolkit presented in Chapter 12.

8.4 Testing Hypotheses with Vignettes

Once test results are back and have been analyzed by the team, what next? We now turn to how prior beliefs should be updated based on these results, how to prototype policies augmented by the behavioral insights informed by them, and how the process then continues, based on iterative testing and learning.

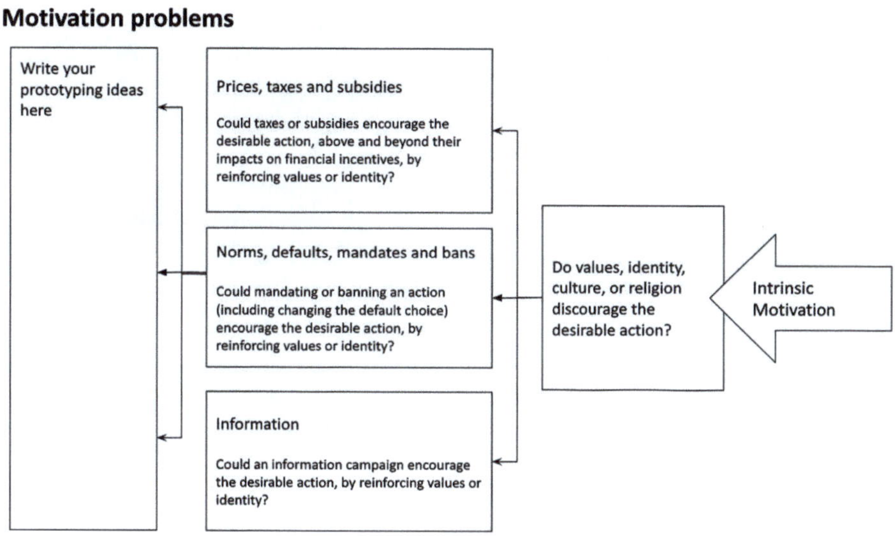

Fig. 8.3 Excerpt from the MSI-PRIx board, focused on real citizens' instrinsic motivation problems. (Source: elaborated by the authors)

8.4.1 Updating Plausibility-Feasibility Ratings

Remember that vignette experiments serve the purpose of refining the team's understanding of the plausibility of different mechanisms. Ultimately, test results should allow us to answer: "Did the experiment confirm or refute the team's hypotheses about which behavioral mechanisms were more or less plausible to our target audience?"

Back to our example, suppose that, in the control scenario, 30% of participants agreed that parents would take their children to prevention services at the health clinic; 60% in the scenario covering limiting mental models; and 80% in the one covering learning through noticing. If that were the case, then the policy team should update beliefs about the relative plausibility of the two behavioral mechanisms: in practice, learning through noticing turned out to be more plausible for explaining the hypothesis of interest than limiting mental models (see Fig. 8.4).

8.4.2 Prototyping Solutions

Given the team's updated understanding about the feasibility and plausibility of the different structural and behavioral mechanisms, the next question is: what is worth prototyping?

It is certainly worth thinking about policies inspired by the most promising behavioral mechanism. In some cases, it may even make sense to think about

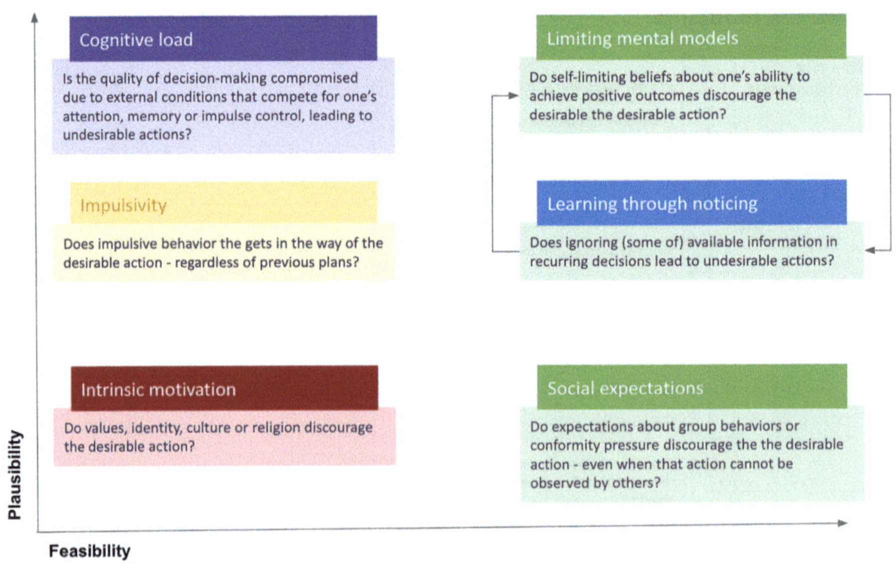

Fig. 8.4 Updating plausibility-feasibility ratings. (Source: elaborated by the authors)

policies that *combine* insights from the most plausible mechanisms with high feasibility. In our example, prototyping should focus on policy tools augmented with insights from learning through noticing and, possibly, also from limiting mental models.

Once the most promising mechanisms have been identified, the PRIx framework should guide the prototyping of public policies augmented by behavioral insights. As we have discussed, different pricing, regulatory, or information policies could address each behavioral mechanism of the MSI framework. In our example, in the case of learning through noticing, subsidies for preventive examinations could reallocate the families' attention to the importance of preventive health care; making prevention compulsory could trigger this same mechanism; information campaigns, in turn, could have the same effects – especially those based on frequent communication.

Which of these policy tools should be prioritized in prototyping? This is a complex question, the answer to which may depend not only on cost-effectiveness considerations, but also, on the policy space in which the policy team is embedded.

Moreover, it might also be relevant to consider structural elements without which policies might be bound to fail. Concretely, in our example, it might make little sense to prototype solutions to boost prevention uptake when it is available for free without including an information campaign that simply makes sure the target audience is aware that preventive health care is indeed available at no costs (a potential structural constraint, as it would affect even the "ideal citizen").

Therefore, the most appealing policy instrument might be an information campaign that combines information about the services that are offered free of charge with strategies to reallocate attention to the concrete benefits of preventive health care, in the hopes of activating learning through noticing. If possible, the campaign should also feature stories of role models who changed their children's lives thanks to prevention uptake, in the hopes of unlocking new mental models amongst the target audience.

As the example illustrates, in this case, behavioral insights did not motivate a policy totally different from others that have been imagined and rolled out in the past. It is less about reinventing policymaking, and more about refining it with better instruments to address the constraints that affect the "real citizen." Campaigns that address not only structural, but also behavioral mechanisms, will be more effective in promoting desirable behaviors – often under the same cost structure for production and dissemination.

In other cases, however, policies inspired by behavioral insights can end up being more disruptive. If, to target limiting mental models, the policy team decides to try out a new logic for routine home visits of health professionals – having role models accompany these visits so as to share their stories with families who are still lagging behind – that would seem like a very odd policy choice to a public manager unaware of the MSI-PRIx framework.

Deciding one way or another might ultimately depend on which policies are most promising within the feasibility space. This decision also hinges on the prototype outcomes.

Prototyping Solutions

Back to the Saudi Arabia case, imagine that, informed by the results of the vignette experiments – which showed that inaccurate social expectations were the key behavioral mechanisms behind husbands' lack of support to their wives' decision to work outside the home – the policy team decided to prototype an information campaign informed by that mechanism.

The prototype was based on a small survey experiment, meant to document the extent to which men's attitudes towards women's work outside the home and their higher-order beliefs (what they believed to be the opinion of others) differed in practice.

Accordingly, study participants were asked to rate the extent to which they agreed with the following claim:

> In my opinion, women should be allowed to work outside of the home.

The same men were then asked to guess the opinion of the other survey participants. The participant who got closest to the right answer would be paid USD 100 at the end of the experiment.

The team found that 72% of participants strictly underestimated the support for female labor outside the home among session participants.

The team then developed a very simple prototype. They shared that statistic with half the participants, and then asked the same two questions to all participants. This simple experiment allowed them to verify that participants changed their higher-order beliefs in response to the intervention.

These findings showcase an opportunity to intervene at that systemic lever, tackling inaccurate social expectations with the help of an information campaign. While the details of the campaign that would make it most effective depend on additional testing (which might progressively increase its fidelity levels), the initial test has validated the merit of the solution.

8.4.3 Back to the Drawing Board

Common sense might suggest that prototyping solutions should be entirely focused on understanding (and perfecting) user experience. In truth, our ability to learn about behavioral mechanisms is always imperfect and iterative. As such, it is possible – and even desirable – that prototyping generates new insights about the mechanisms at play in this context, and that this ends up taking the policy team back to the drawing board.

Have we identified all structural and behavioral mechanisms that are highly feasible and highly plausible to our working hypothesis? And so begins a new cycle of screening mechanisms (with the help of the MSI framework), testing (possibly, with the help of vignettes), refining insights, rethinking solutions (with the help of the PRIx framework), and prototyping.

In our preventive health care example, the information campaign prototype may end up generating poor results, for reasons above and beyond the limited user experience of the low-fidelity prototype. Imagine that, in practice, the channel chosen to broadcast the campaign (e.g., television) is embedded in a context of cognitive load – because the target audience tends to watch TV at the end of the day, when they get home tired from work. In such a context, addressing cognitive load may be a necessary condition for the success of the information campaign. Because the policy team had agreed that cognitive load is not very amenable to policy interventions, that insight might lead them to redirect their approach. That might mean merely choosing a new policy instrument, or it might mean entirely shifting from focusing on an inattention problem (learning through noticing) to a self-control problem (limiting mental models) in face of the challenges of overcoming other constraints on the target audience's limited mental bandwidth.

As this discussion hopefully makes it obvious, it is impossible to anticipate the end of this process, in an attempt to skip steps. Iterative testing and learning, and being open to change your mind, are the most important ingredients for evidence-based policymaking in general, and particularly so when combining behavioral sciences with systemic design.

Summary

1. This chapter introduced a practical guide for identifying the structural and behavioral mechanisms relevant to the public problem at hand.
2. We have seen that the starting point for an effective behavioral diagnostics is to ensure that the problem is properly mapped, with the systems and (even better) subsystems clearly identified.
3. We learned that the subsystems are an important part of a precise diagnosis, as they illustrate various opportunities for intervention through policy tools at different points in the system.
4. After that, it is important to define the hypothesis on which the policy theory of change will be based. The hypothesis will not always be precise at first, but it is important to address only one hypothesis at a time.
5. Once the hypothesis has been identified, the next step is to define the structural and behavioral mechanisms that will be tested. Even when focusing on a single problem, the number of potential behavioral mechanisms can still be very large. As such, it is important to select the more plausible and feasible mechanisms – the ones that motivate solutions that could actually be implemented in this context.
6. We also introduced vignette experiments, designed to refine the team's understanding of the plausibility of different feasible mechanisms.
7. Lastly, given the policy team's understanding of the feasibility of the different mechanisms, and their updated beliefs about the plausibility of each, it should start to plan which policies are worth prototyping. This process should be informed by the PRIx framework.
8. It is also important to go back to basics. At the end of each step, even as the prototype is being tested, the team must constantly ask themselves: are the hypothesis and the mechanisms right and precise? It is important to always question the assumptions and iterate in order to find the policies that can really influence real citizens' behaviors.

Suggested Readings

Behavioral Sciences and Public Policies: the use of SIMPLES MENTE in innovation projects" (GNOVA, 2020)

EIFLER, Stefanie; PETZOLD, Knut. Validity aspects of vignette experiments: Expected "what-if" differences between reports of behavioral intentions and actual behavior. Experimental methods in survey research: Techniques that combine random sampling with random assignment, p. 393-416, 2019.

STEINER, Peter M., ATZMÜLLER, Christiane, SU, Dan. Designing valid and reliable vignette experiments for survey research: A case study on the fair gender income gap. Journal of Methods and Measurement in the Social Sciences, v. 7, n. 2, p. 52-94, 2016.

Chapter 9
Best Practices in Testing Behavioral Mechanisms

Just like almost anything, running effective vignettes experiments requires trial, error, repeat. This chapter compiles best practices and the most common mistakes in implementing them to inform the do's and don'ts of this iterative learning process.

9.1 Include Enough Details to Generate Identification with the Target Audience

The rationale behind vignettes is that interviewees should identify with the characters portrayed in them, in the hopes of indirectly eliciting their beliefs and intentions without triggering social desirability biases. Lack of identification might either fail to get around such biases or, even when that is not the case, fail to gauge reliable information from the target audience.

Tip
The vignette story (and its accompanying visual elements, if any) should describe the characters – their traits, their background – in some detail, so as to increase the likelihood of having participants identify with them.

Back to our example of limited use of preventive health care among poor families, the vignette might begin by describing the main character: "Maria, a single mother with two small children, lives on just enough income to keep her small business running and to buy just the basics for her children." If the income profile of the target audience is different, or if their typical family structure is different, then the vignette should try to incorporate these elements.

G. Lichand et al., *Behavioral Insights for Policy Design*,
https://doi.org/10.1007/978-3-031-33034-6_9

9.2 Avoid *Too Much* Detail, So as Not to Distract Interviewees from the Mechanisms of Interest

Vignettes that are too long, with intricate details that are not relevant for producing identification with the target audience nor for describing the mechanisms of interest that are the object of the test, might end up distracting participants, making the experimental results noisier.

Tip
It should take no longer than 5 min for interviewees to absorb the story portrayed in each vignette.

9.3 Prefer Few Scenarios and More Interviews to Many Scenarios and Few Interviews

Each person reacts to a story differently. We only start learning about patterns when we compare differences across many interviews – with large numbers, idiosyncratic factors balance out. In the early stages of diagnostics, however, the ability of the policy team to run a large number of interviews is typically limited. For that reason, it is better to test less mechanisms, making interviews shorter, to be able to include more participants.

Tip
If the team can do only a few interviews, it is better to test only a few mechanisms. Thinking carefully about hypotheses, plausibility, and feasibility is key to focusing testing on what really matters.

Start with only two scenarios per participant: the control scenario and a modified scenario. With many respondents, that setup still allows for testing several mechanisms – having the modified scenario change across participants (ideally, by random assignment).

Based on our experience, in the early stages of experimentation, 10–15 interviews per mechanism can be enough to provide valuable insights for behavioral diagnostics.

9.4 Beware of Biasing Responses When Explaining the Survey Objectives

Before starting an interview, it is best practice – as part of the process of obtaining informed consent – to explain the goals of the survey to participants. In the case of vignette experiments, however, since a key objective is to generate identification without inducing social desirability biases, it is better not to be too specific about what you want to achieve. After all, if the interviewee understands that, by talking about the character, he is talking about him or herself, the advantage of the indirect elicitation technique is lost.

Tip

Instead of briefing participants in full detail *ex ante*, it is best to debrief *ex post*. Lead with a more general description; in our example, that might be: "Our goal is to understand what might affect the family's decision to use preventive health care." Then, at the very end of the interview, review its more specific objectives – only after all the answers have been collected. Debriefing prevents deception, as it allows participants to withdraw their responses if they feel like they no longer want to participate in the research. Failing to do that would amount to a violation of participants' autonomy, a core principle of research ethics.

9.5 Start with the Control Scenario

If all participants answer questions for the control scenario and at least one more, comparisons can always be made within respondent. This helps parse out differences in responses across different scenarios that simply reflect idiosyncratic differences in the profile of respondents assigned to each of them. With few interviews, the statistical properties of the tests are not ideal, making it more important to ensure direct comparability.

Tip

If only a few interviews have been conducted (which is common, especially in the early diagnostic phase), the most important consideration is to ensure that every interviewee responds first to the control scenario, and then to at least one modified scenario.

9.6 Vary Only the Essentials Across Scenarios

It is tempting to present modified scenarios that tell stories completely different from the control version. After all, if a character has a different mental model, say, she probably also makes several other different choices, or has other characteristics consistent with this mental model. Nevertheless, incorporating all those differences would be ultimately detrimental to testing: if we observe differences in responses between the control and modified versions, it will be difficult to interpret whether this is because limiting mental models are a promising behavioral in this context or, rather, because one of these other contextual elements is very relevant for the problem in question.

Tip
Vary only the essentials between the control and modified scenarios, so as to isolate the structural or behavioral mechanism from other factors. The questionnaire that follows each scenario must also be *identical* across all versions – otherwise, we cannot assess whether responses change across scenarios! This implies that in the case where a respondent is exposed to multiple scenarios, he or she will answer each question multiple times.

9.7 Do Not Leave Out High-Feasibility Structural Mechanisms

It may be tempting to focus entirely on behavioral mechanisms in vignette experiments, especially when they are new to the public manager's toolkit. The truth is, however, that many persistent public problems are fundamentally affected by structural mechanisms, that is, they would generate vicious cycles even for the "ideal citizen."

Tip
Back to our example, the structural scenario could add, for instance, that "Maria received a letter from the Ministry of Health explaining that children who undergo preventive exams tend to miss *X* school days less than those who do not, saving their families USD *X* per year in emergency expenses." – where the *X*'s should be filled in with the statistics relevant to the target population.

In our example, inaccurate beliefs about the future returns of taking up preventive health care probably also contribute to explain their low utilization even when available at no cost. Since that structural mechanism is very amenable to information campaigns, its feasibility is high. As such, it might be useful to test a scenario that incorporates this mechanism.

Besides reflecting an important policy that may not yet be in place, this structural vignette helps to understand how important behavioral mechanisms are in comparison. For instance, suppose that 30% of respondents answer that the family would use preventive health in the control scenario, as opposed to 45% in the scenario focused on limiting mental models. Is this figure high – an increase in adoption equivalent to half its original prevalence? Or, rather, low – still less than half of the potential adoption? Adding a structural scenario might help *benchmark* those figures. If adoption in that structural scenario were, say, 50%, then 45% in the scenario with limiting mental models might seem quite high, pointing out this mechanism is nearly as relevant as a structural factor. If, conversely, the estimated adoption rate in the structural scenario were, say, 90%, then the natural conclusion would be that the behavioral mechanism is less plausible in this context – at least for the purpose of augmenting the public manager tool kit relative to the policies that were already available.

9.8 Ask About the Character's Beliefs and Feelings

It is useful to begin the questionnaire after the vignettes by asking about what the character portrayed in them thinks, and how he or she feels. This not only helps triggering empathy and identification, but also, it can help assess the plausibility of the mechanism by allowing the policy team to follow the theory of change leading to the (un)desirable behaviors as they compare responses across scenarios.

> **Tip**
> Back to our example, the questionnaire might ask "How does Maria feel when she thinks about her children's future?" and "What does she think she should set as priority for her household spending next month?"

9.9 Ask About Desirable Behaviors

Even if thoughts and feelings are important, it is critical to ask about the behaviors of interest in the questionnaire. The reason is that while certain mechanisms might seem relevant when we look at the former, these might ultimately exert little influence when it comes to the latter. When a mechanism is associated with both attitudes and behaviors consistently across scenarios, then we can be more confident that the vignette experiment has captured a useful insight.

Tip
Back to our example, the questionnaire could ask "How likely is it that Maria would take her children to the health center for preventive exams at least twice a year?" or "Maria's children are healthy, do not complain of any symptoms, and she does not notice anything different about them. Would she still take them to the health center for preventive exams?"

9.10 Be Careful Not to Induce Responses with the Vignette Itself

A common mistake in experiments with vignettes is to already include feelings, thoughts, and actions in the description itself. That tends to trigger social desirability bias, precisely what this elicitation technique seeks to avert.

Tip
In our example, saying that "Maria does not believe that prevention is better than treatment" would probably already induce the interviewee to state that Maria is unlikely to take her children for preventive examinations.

9.11 Avoid Most Binary Questions

The risk of including only binary questions is that they do not allow respondents to express the intensity of their agreement or disagreement, reducing the scope for variability in their answers across scenarios.

Tip
While it is okay to include some binary questions, prefer questions that allow participants to express intensity. This can be done using scales. In our example, the questionnaire could state: "Among the alternatives below, please rank Maria's worries from 1 to 5, where 1 is her biggest worry and 5 is her least worry." Alternatively: "From 0 to 100, how likely is it that Mary will take her children for checkups next month."

Another possibility is to offer qualitative alternatives. For instance, "Which of the following sentences best describes what Maria thinks," where each of them addresses different reasons for why she might not take her children to preventive exams even when they are available for free.

9.12 Ask About Willingness to Engage in Costly Actions

Even though vignette experiments are a preferred alternative to asking subjects directly what they would do, this method is not completely immune to social desirability biases (even when following all best practices in this chapter). Another complementary approach is to ask individuals directly about their willingness to engage in real-life actions – not the behavior of interest, but one related to its overarching theme. If engagement is costly, these costs should tone down desirability pressures.

Tip

Start by sticking to the vignette background story: ask how the respondent thinks the character would behave when it comes to undertaking costly actions to support that overarching theme. In our example, the questionnaire could ask: "If Maria had the chance to allocate *X* minutes per week to convince her neighbor to take her children for preventive exams at the health center, how many minutes would she commit?"

The questionnaire could follow by asking the respondent about their *own* willingness to commit in real life, outside of the vignette: "How about you? If we were to organize a real mobilization campaign, how many minutes would you be willing to commit per week to try to convince families like Maria's to undertake preventive health care?"

Changes in the level of commitment across the different scenarios can be very informative about the relative importance of each mechanism, especially as the action involves costs (direct or indirect, because of the opportunity cost of time). The direct question, in turn, adds a greater degree of realism, while the costs to the action – if perceived as indeed real – might be effective in toning down social desirability biases. After all, if that is the case, then agreeableness is no longer *cheap talk.*

9.13 Beware of Floor and Ceiling Effects in the Control Scenario

If all respondents agree (disagree) with a question in the control scenario, then there is no way to learn what mechanisms could increase (decrease) the prevalence of that attitude or behavior in the modified scenarios.

Tip

Try to ensure that each question induces enough variation in survey responses to prevent such ceiling or floor effects in the control scenario. One strategy might be adding additional categories to allow respondents to express finer-grain intensity of their perceptions. Another might be adding new qualitative statements that is somewhat close to the one chosen by (nearly) all respondents, but changing it slightly to emphasize a competing mechanism.

9.14 Pretest the Vignettes and Questionnaire with Your Target Audience

Pretesting means simulating the test ahead of time, at a smaller scale. This is often used as an opportunity to evaluate critical aspects of the questionnaire before it goes live (such as the presence of ceiling or floor effects just discussed), and while there is still time to change it. Moreover, pretests can also help assess whether the different scenarios are capturing the essential elements of the mechanisms they should be focused on – despite small numbers, with the help of qualitative interviews.

Tip

The pretest should allow answering the following questions: Does the questionnaire suffer from ceiling or floor effects in the control scenario? Do the modified scenarios seem to change responses in the expected direction in each case? Do respondents understand each question? Could survey questions be rephrased or simplified (e.g., when asking about probabilities)?

It is essential that the pretest is conducted with members of the target audience of the subsequent vignette experiment. It is of no use if public managers understand the questionnaire perfectly, but the target audience of the policy does not.

You may need to conduct several rounds of pretests: test, adjust, retest. It is better to spend time making sure that the experiment really captures what we need, rather than spending time and resources collecting data that will not ultimately be informative.

9.15 Avoid "Group Work"

Lastly, a common mistake is to interview more than one person at a time. This tends to generate useless results: when respondents discuss among themselves, they tend to activate meta-cognition processes that induce them to lose identification with the characters portrayed in the vignette. Moreover, group work can generate other biases link to in-group behavior and social expectations (mechanisms we discussed in previous chapters).

Tip
Each interviewee should respond individually, and no one other than the survey team should be able to observe him or her throughout the process. This is why the policy team cannot mindlessly delegate the implementation of the survey experiment; in face of the best practices and common mistakes discussed in this chapter, it is crucial to closely monitor how vignettes are presented and how the questionnaire is applied.

Summary
1. This chapter compiled best practices and common mistakes for using vignette experiments to learn about plausible structural and behavioral mechanisms behind the social problem at hand.
2. Effective vignettes make interviewees identify with the characters portrayed in them, in the hopes of indirectly eliciting their beliefs and intentions without triggering social desirability biases.
3. In contrast, poorly designed vignettes fail at gauging reliable information from the target audience.
4. In this chapter, we highlighted some of the best practices for designing effective vignette experiments. In particular, design short questionnaires, test few mechanisms at a time, and pretest extensively.
5. We also indicate the most common mistakes when conducting vignette experiments. In particular, avoid descriptions that might trigger social desirability biases, avoid questions that induce specific responses, and do not interview respondents together.
6. Although based on our extensive experience, the most important advice is to consider what the policy team needs to learn and under what time and budget constraints. Adapt experimentation with those goals and constraints in mind, informed by these tips.
7. When designing vignette experiments, we are also subject to our own biases. That is why it is so critical to pretest – especially with the target audience of the policy itself – to ensure that they can capture the phenomena we are ultimately interested in.

Suggested Readings

Harrits, G. S., & Møller, M. Ø. (2021). Qualitative Vignette Experiments: A Mixed Methods Design. Journal of Mixed Methods Research, 15(4), 526–545. https://doi.org/10.1177/1558689820977607

Freedman G, Seidman M, Flanagan M, Green MC, Kaufman G. Updating a Classic: A New Generation of Vignette Experiments Involving Iterative Decision Making. Advances in Methods and Practices in Psychological Science. 2018;1(1):43-59. doi:https://doi.org/10.1177/2515245917742982

Hainmueller, Jens & Hangartner, Dominik & Yamamoto, Teppei. (2015). Validating Vignette and Conjoint Survey Experiments Against Real-World Behavior. Proceedings of the National Academy of Sciences of the United States of America. 112. https://doi.org/10.1073/pnas.1416587112.

Sheringham, J., Kuhn, I. & Burt, J. The use of experimental vignette studies to identify drivers of variations in the delivery of healthcare: a scoping review. BMC Med Res Methodol 21, 81 (2021). https://doi.org/10.1186/s12874-021-01247-4

Steiner, Peter M. et al. "Designing Valid and Reliable Vignette Experiments for Survey Research: A Case Study on the Fair Gender Income Gap." Journal of Methods and Measurement in the Social Sciences 7 (2017): 52-94.

Chapter 10
Designing for Heterogeneous Types

10.1 Does Everyone Suffer from the Same Biases?

When we explain why the real citizen's choices deviate from those of the ideal citizen, we typically appeal to general features of the human psyche. Limited mental bandwidth implies that *every individual* faces limited attention, executive memory, and self-control. While external conditions might make these constraints more important for some (e.g., financial worries capture part of the available bandwidth, magnifying inattention and self-control problems among the poor), biases such as inattention, procrastination, and limiting mental models should, in principle, apply equally to all individuals once differences in their external environment (e.g., their material conditions) are accounted for. Similarly, evolutionary forces imply that *every individual* is sensitive to internal conflicts between rationality and affect, to peer pressure, and to social image concerns.

The conceptual generality of the psychological and evolutionary forces behind behavioral biases often leads researchers and practitioners to think that interventions to address them should target all individuals alike. The truth, however, is that such general forces combine with each individual's *unique background* and experiences to produce a rich distribution of behaviors.

Concretely, more often than not less than half of subjects will display any particular behavioral bias in elicitations conducted as part of lab experiments, or even outside the lab. Even for celebrated biases such as present bias (the tendency to procrastinate) or the common ratio effect (the tendency to choose a sure option instead of a lottery, but then to switch to a riskier lottery over a safer one once all probabilities of nonzero outcomes are scaled down by the same common ratio), typically no more than 40% of experimental subjects display behaviors consistent with those biases.

What does that imply for the potential of behaviorally informed policies to change behaviors of the real citizen? It suggests that, when such interventions are

G. Lichand et al., *Behavioral Insights for Policy Design*,
https://doi.org/10.1007/978-3-031-33034-6_10

not adapted to the specific circumstances of the recipient, they are unlikely to produce large aggregate effects. Interestingly, such insight might both help explain the recent demise of governmental nudge units – which have largely ignored heterogeneity and its implications throughout – and come to their rescue. If they could effectively *screen behavioral types*, to accurately target the right intervention to the right citizen, then nudge units would likely unlock the promise of large impacts for behavioral insights within the public sector – the one that captured hearts and minds as nudge units were rapidly expanding in the mid-2010s.

Naturally, that would also bring about new challenges, from the need for scientific evidence on the likely sources of heterogeneity, to the ethical dilemmas of having governments screen individual biases and target them with interventions, to the opportunities and perils of technology for adaptive experimentation. We cover these issues in the remainder of this chapter.

Before that, we start by providing examples of how heterogeneity plays out in each of the behavioral mechanisms of the MSI framework.

10.2 Heterogeneous Motivation Problems

One of the easiest ways to think about heterogeneity is when it comes to misinformation. Partly, misinformation can be understood as a structural mechanism: even the ideal citizen would make suboptimal choices under inaccurate beliefs about the costs of or returns to certain decisions. Nonetheless, misinformation can also result from a variety of behavioral mechanisms, including selectively disregarding evidence because of cognitive dissonance (which, as discussed, can be thought of as a manifestation of the desire to be consistent with one's internal beliefs systems, part of what we characterize as intrinsic motivation, even in face of information that contradicts them).

Different initial beliefs, combined with different trajectories of exposure to new information, might easily lead to large heterogeneity in how accurate different individuals are at any given point in time – and the more so in the presence of cognitive dissonance.

Some of these wrong beliefs might apply to the costs of or returns to private decisions, whose outcomes can only be observed by the decision-maker. In turn, other inaccurate beliefs might apply to decisions with public consequences. In particular, some of those might be what economists call higher-order beliefs, in that they are beliefs about what others do, or about what others expected them to do – what we have characterized as social expectations.

We already discussed extensively how inaccurate social expectations can lead real citizens to act to their disadvantage. If there is heterogeneity, however, some will be more likely to act on those beliefs than others. Strikingly, it might even be that some individuals underestimate the true prevalence of a certain behavior, while others overestimate it. In the example of female labor force participation in Saudi Arabia, it is in fact the case that while most men underestimate the share of other husbands who would support their wives if they were to work outside of home, more than a few overestimate it.

Accordingly, an intervention that disclosed the true rate of support for female labor force participation moved beliefs and behaviors by different magnitudes (and even in different directions!) depending on each subject's prior beliefs. In other words, the intervention affected different citizens to different extents, precisely because of heterogeneity. Its largest impacts were concentrated on those who started with beliefs far off from the true rate of support for female labor force participation, while those who were already accurate to start with were, unsurprisingly, barely affected.

10.3 Heterogenous Self-Control Problems

Limiting mental models likely arise from a combination of frustrating prior experiences, limited affordances, and limited mental bandwidth during the execution of the task at hand. Concretely, a student might display a fixed mindset (beliefs that intelligence is fixed and that there is nothing one could do to change it) in math classes because of a history of bad grades, because of parents who did not believe that she could succeed in math and/or because of a former teacher who kept emphasizing that learning math was a matter of talent rather than effort. Such a fixed mindset is likely to be more pronounced when the student is tired after a long day at school or after an intense weekend of prep work, when her mental bandwidth is lower – limiting her ability to exercise self-control.

Variation in prior experiences, family backgrounds, exposure to teachers, and external conditions taxing mental bandwidth, all combine to induce a rich distribution of mental states, including mindsets. In a striking example, a study in Brazil as public schools had just reopened in the aftermath of the pandemic documented that roughly 50% of secondary students displayed beliefs consistent with a fixed mindset: they agreed that if they were not good at math, they would never be good at it. While relatively wealthier students were less likely to express a fixed mindset, at least 30% among the poorest students still displayed a growth mindset, and at least 40% among the wealthiest students still displayed a fixed mindset.

Unsurprisingly, an intervention to promote a growth mindset through text messages to students and their families only worked in schools where most students were characterized by a fixed mindset. Heterogeneity was, once again, key.

10.4 Heterogeneous Inattention Problems

Similarly, variations in mental bandwidth due to differences in external circumstances likely induce a rich distribution of behavioral biases linked to inattention as well. This applies to a wide range of perceptual biases associated with limited attention; in particular, sensitivity to anchoring (the tendency to react to salient features of the choice architecture, especially when it comes to recent information, likely as a result of recency bias and the availability heuristic). The prevalence and intensity of such bias has been recently shown to vary systematically across individuals.

The evidence goes as follows. A study in Malawi offered individuals the opportunity to buy preventive health care goods at different prices. A couple of weeks later, those individuals received a new visit from the sales person, offering them a new opportunity to purchase the same and other preventive health care products. The study found that some individuals were much more likely than others to react to past prices when specifying how much they would be willing to pay. Concretely, some of those who saw lower prices were not just more likely to express a lower willingness to pay; they offered exactly the same price as they had seen in the recent past – consistent with anchoring. For others, however, seeing lower prices made no difference to their subsequent willingness to pay.

On one hand, this creates a policy challenge: past discounts affect different individuals in very different ways. For those who do not anchor on low prices seen in the past, discounts induce higher purchases in the present without compromising future demand. Conversely, for those who anchor, the higher purchases induced by discounts today at least partly offset future purchases. Because take-up of preventive health care has positive externalities, anchoring leads to socially inefficient outcomes. Because poverty tends to magnify inattention (and, hence, anchoring) through cognitive load, heterogeneity likely accentuates social inequalities.

On the other hand, this also creates policy opportunities: if individual types could be accurately screened, and if pricing could be successfully targeted to different types, then a government that wants to maximize take-up might offer higher-than-average discounts to individuals who are largely insensitive to anchoring, and lower discounts to anchoring types. We discuss screening and targeting, their technical requirements, their implications for social inequalities, and their ethical implications, in the next section.

10.5 Screening

What would it look like to have government screen behavioral types? That would require governments to be able to identify who suffers from which problem. There are three key issues that we must address: feasibility, stability, and best practices.

The very first question is whether it is even feasible to identify ahead of time who is most likely to suffer from motivation, self-control, or inattention problems. To illustrate that the answer is positive, let us look into behavioral biases in financial decisions. In this domain, when individuals fail to act in accordance with the ideal citizen, the costs are immediate, and it is hard to reconcile deviations with alternative explanations that would rescue such "mistakes" as rational. A striking example is that of individuals who check their account balance less often when it is low or negative, or their portfolio account less often after they have experienced recent losses (a bias known as the "ostrich effect"). Information avoidance can be rationalized, for instance, by individuals updating their beliefs about their own worth once they acknowledge losses – consistent with what we have classified as intrinsic motivation problems, or anticipating that such losses will trigger cognitive load – consistent with inattention problems. Is it possible to anticipate who displays ostrich effects in real-life financial decisions? A study in Iceland found that individuals who log in on a financial management app multiple times a day at payday (which is inconsistent with information motives, since all information could have already been processed the first time around) are precisely the ones who are less likely to log in when their account is low or negative. In other words, login behavior during payday is a feasible way to screen for ostrich effects throughout the month.

A potential drawback of that example is that governments might not have access to the relevant data (such as from financial management apps), especially in low- and middle-income countries, where most transactions might be offline for a large share of their population. Two other examples illustrate that there are ways to make progress towards screening types even in the absence of high-frequency data on individual financial decisions. Another study in Iceland documents that surveys to elicit economic preferences and decision-making ability can accurately predict real-life demand for high-cost loans. A study in the USA, in turn, shows that take-up of long-term care insurance can be predicted by survey responses that elicit narrow framing (the tendency to favor safe options in the domain of gains, but risky options in the domain of losses).

If predicting real-life biases is feasible even with lab-type survey measures, government could proceed in two ways: either running a survey with every eligible citizen for a particular policy – which seems daunting – or, alternatively, with a representative sample that allows one to identify individual characteristics that correlate with the survey answers that help predict the behavioral type of interest. In effect, the US study was embedded in the annual Health and Retirement Survey, which is nationally representative of Americans over the age of 50. As such, this survey could be used by the government to inform the screening of individuals unlikely to demand long-term care insurance based on characteristics that it can observe for all citizens – such as age, race, income, and education. That of course brings about additional concerns, to which we return in our discussion of targeting below.

Since even adding a module to a representative survey is costly, how often should governments do it? The answer depends on our second issue, that of stability: how likely an individual is to display the same bias over time or, most importantly – in face of the feasibility constraints just discussed – how stable is the correlation between characteristics and underlying behavioral types?

This is not an easy question to answer. Only a few studies measure behavioral biases repeatedly over time. Those studies tend to find reasonably low persistence for specific biases, but larger persistence for indices that capture a multiplicity of biases at the same time. Such a pattern is consistent with measurement error: any given choice is subject to a range of contextual factors unrelated to underlying preferences or biases, which might affect how individuals respond to it. When many choices are considered together, measurement error can be (at least partially) parsed out. "Behavioral indices" that combine multiple survey measures of biases seem to be a promising avenue to obtain a stable measure of decision-making quality – or, put another way, deviations from the ideal citizen's decisions – and of the association between the latter and individual characteristics.

If screening is feasible and can be made economical – through representative surveys that do not have to be constantly conducted, in face of stability – then the final issue we have to discuss is how to best screen for biases within each mechanism of the MSI matrix. There again, the research is only nascent.

When it comes to motivation, for issues such as inaccurate social expectations, measuring heterogeneity depends on assessing the difference between prior beliefs and the true prevalence in the target population. While it might be intuitive that merely asking subjects to report what they think the actual prevalence is would yield truthful answers, there are many reasons why that might ultimately fail – some simple, like difficulties in understanding probabilities, some more complex, such as social desirability bias (whereby subjects might want to conform to surveyor's expectations by providing the "right answer"). Accurately and truthfully eliciting beliefs might depend on a combination of incentives – paying those who get the true prevalence right – and designing the survey instruments to make sure probabilities and incentives are well understood – which requires careful design to the target audience and extensive piloting. Several studies in low-income countries resort to visual representations of probabilities, and validation tasks to ensure participants understand before moving on to the actual elicitation.

For other motivation problems, accurate elicitation might require even more complex surveying techniques. Measuring intrinsic motivations might require implicit association tests (IAT), which track subjects' response times to understand biases that even the individual him or herself might be unable to actively recognize. Concretely, these tests often take the form of binary choices on a tablet screen. Subjects have to press left or right, depending on the prompt. In a recent study, researchers had teachers press the side of the screen with the positive word. Words would come up in pairs (e.g., war and peace, whereby one should press the side of the screen where peace shows up). In different rounds, pictures would show up along with the words, portraying a national or an immigrant student. While, in principle, pictures should not influence the way individuals responded to the prompts, whether the picture was "congruent" or not with the positive word tends to make individuals faster or slower, depending on how they implicitly associate each picture with positive emotions. Teachers who tend to discriminate against immigrant students (as measured by differential treatment in the classroom, including grading, relative to standardized tests, which are centrally graded) also tended to slow down more when faced with incongruencies (when positive words were matched to the picture of the immigrant student). It is not easy to design such tests. Even though they can be made simpler when one is only interested in the joint distribution of the implicit biases and observable characteristics, it is likely best to work with researchers. Similarly, accurately capturing sensitivity to social pressure often requires experiments: in that case, to track how individual answers change when they can be publicly visible or not, like the ones we discussed in the case of women's career ambitions within the University of Chicago MBA class.

When it comes to screening self-control problems, two different approaches have been used by researchers. First, elicitation of demand for commitment strategies. If individuals are sophisticated about their self-control problems – that is, if they anticipate that they will fail to follow through on their past plans – then they should be willing to pay to remove their ability to deviate from those plans in the future. There are two challenges with that strategy. First, along the lines of our previous discussion, there is a multiplicity of technical challenges involved in accurately and truthfully eliciting preferences. Recent studies show that binary elicitation of demand for commitment is extremely prone to measurement error. The alternative, eliciting willingness to pay for commitment, is hard to implement – especially in low-income settings. Second, demand for costly commitment tends to be very low even among sophisticated subjects, precisely because those who procrastinate tend to overweight the present relative to the future, making them less inclined to agree to incur costs in the present in exchange for future benefits. An alternative is to design commitment strategies whose costs are only in the future, like "Save More Tomorrow," which we previously discussed. Nonetheless, demand for this type of program might overstate the share of present-biased individuals, not only because it might be challenging to process the expected costs and benefits of committing to such a strategy in the future, but also, because this decision might be reversed later (which is documented by recent studies).

For other commitment problems, such as parent bias, demand for commitment also tends to be low; only in that case because these parents tend to be too optimistic about the extent to which they will not reallocate from their children towards themselves in the future. Delaying commitment costs to the future has no conceptual bearing in that case.

In face of these challenges, researchers have turned to a second approach: lab-type experiments to capture procrastination, which can be conducted as part of surveys. These experiments present subjects with a series of decisions in which they have to trade-off resources over time, changing the horizon at which these trade-offs are evaluated – some, between two future periods; others, between a future period and the present, precisely to capture discontinuities in how present payoffs are evaluated by present-biased individuals. This is not without its own challenges: such choices must not only be incentivized, but also, must involve real consumption or effort tasks (because issues such as distrust in future payments and the fungibility of money can generate odd behaviors, sometimes leading to completely wrong inference about time preferences). Once again, this is challenging and should be done in partnership with researchers.

In the case of limiting mental models, we are still in the early days of measurement. There are some widely used surveys to capture psychological constructs such as a fixed mindset, but it is still unclear what these instruments capture exactly. Ongoing work uses machine learning techniques to extract from writing samples or dialogue between students, teachers and parents, the terms and expressions most predictive of behavior consistent with each mental model in the classroom and with desirable educational outcomes. We still have to see the extent to which these efforts will be fruitful, and to which they will ultimately rescue the typical survey instruments, or eventually lead to new ones, to inform government efforts to measure mental models and the characteristics that correlate with them.

Last, when it comes to screening inattention problems, survey instruments typically borrow tasks from the cognitive psychology literature, assessing the extent to which subjects' decisions change with the framing of alternatives, as in some of the examples we have discussed before. As in the previous cases, getting these questions just right tends to require both technical expertise and extensive piloting, and is best done in collaboration with researchers.

10.6 Targeting

Assuming governments could perfectly screen behavioral types, what is next? Targeting different types with different policies would require governments to be able to personalize them, effectively offering a menu of interventions and dosages – at the limit, to target each citizen with the right intervention for him or her. In this section, we discuss whether targeting policies would be feasible within the public sector's institutional constraints, the potential role of technology, its implications for social inequalities, and the new ethical dilemmas it would bring about.

First, when it comes to institutional constraints to policy personalization, governments already offer a range of custom policies, based on citizens' characteristics – which determine whether individuals are eligible to certain benefits. Unemployment insurance is only targeted at those who lost their jobs recently; conditional cash transfers are only targeted at those below a certain threshold of income and assets; remedial education is only targeted at those with low enough grades or coming from disadvantaged backgrounds.

Above and beyond targeting one's economic conditions or educational history, many governments also promote targeted policies based on traits. Concretely, increasingly common affirmative action policies enforce employment mandates for citizens with disabilities, for women in male-dominated positions, and for people of color in white-dominated industries. The challenge of targeting behavioral types is that, different from those other characteristics, types are *not visible*. Concretely, a government might propose that, for example, some citizens should be eligible for larger discounts than others, not because they belong to a particular social group or because of their recent history – even if those characteristics are correlated with types and, hence, are used in combination to screen who should be targeted – but, rather, because of their underlying motivation, self-control, and/or inattention problems.

In most countries, it is still a gray area of public sector legislation whether one could legally prevent access to certain policies based on features that are not verifiable. The truth is that, in practice, discrimination based on invisible features already happens in many core dimensions of life. In the private sector, from banks to insurance providers, individuals are priced out or outright denied services based on their predicted types. The bank or the insurer does not have to provide a justification for charging different customers different prices, and the bank is not legally challenged upon declining a loan request. All this happens within the legal spectrum. In the public sector, however, even though most constitutions stipulate that government has to abide to the principle of isonomy, whereby all equal individuals should be treated equally before the law and the unequal must be treated differently in the same proportion of their inequality, defining and measuring what inequality means is a hard ask when it comes to complex phenomena such as behavioral biases. Nonetheless, when a government hires a private provider, like an educational technology startup, that startup might use algorithms to target different content to different public school students based on their predicted types. Is that legal or illegal?

To try to circumvent these legal constraints, an alternative way to target without being discriminatory would be to have citizens self-select into different programs, based on what each of them considers most advantageous for him or her. Concretely, many governments offer food subsidies, such as food stamps, for all those willing to wait long enough in line. In principle, all citizens are eligible to that benefit; in practice, only few are willing to wait long enough in line – presumably, those with the highest expected benefits from it and/or with the lowest opportunity costs of time.

The last qualifier is revealing: relying on citizens to self-screen into the program will attract the right types only to the extent that the screening mechanism selects on the relevant dimension. We already discussed that, for a variety of reasons, it is unlikely that demand for commitment strategies would be high among even sophisticated individuals who suffer from self-control problems. The same is likely to apply to the other mechanisms of the MSI framework. Inattentive subjects are unlikely to notice that a policy might be available to support them. Motivation problems might work against self-screening unless most citizens suffer from that problem (making screening far less useful to start with).

All in all, effective targeting behavior types will likely require changes in the current legislation. It might be that the data and algorithms used to predict eligibility will have to be validated by external committees before they can become effective. Behavioral scientists and legislators will have to work closely to ensure that the benefits of targeting policies to behavioral types are in fact greater than its potential costs.

Among these potential costs are implications for social inequalities. Our example of targeted discounts for preventive health care illustrates the dilemma. Even if targeting effectively maximizes take-up of preventive health care over time (by trading off the current and future effects of discounts accounting for the fact that some citizens might be sensitive to anchoring), in practice the latter will pay a higher price for the same good. Since, as extensively discussed, poverty tends to accentuate behavioral biases by taxing one's cognitive bandwidth, then the poor will tend to pay higher prices if the policy targets exclusively based on behavioral types.

This discussion suggests that a policymaker concerned with both addressing externalities and promoting social justice will have to balance both considerations when thinking about optimal targeting. In that example, this could be done explicitly, by ensuring that the poor pay, on average, a lower price, but varying price within the income category, based on predicted behavioral types.

When targeting is possible, technology could help unlock much larger impacts of personalization. The reason is that, per our discussion in the previous section, governments can only screen inefficiently in the absence of individual data – by leveraging the correlation between observable characteristics and behavioral biases in representative surveys. If, however, governments could access high-frequency data on how citizens react to different policies, then it could improve screening quality over time. Concretely, a recent study shows that, in Brazilian secondary schools, sending text messages to students and their families to promote a growth mindset in the aftermath of the pandemic led to large average improvements in test scores. Researchers tested six versions of the intervention – emphasizing different aspects of the growth mindset message, for example, that school effort has high returns, the importance of weighing the future heavily, or the value of taking risks. Most importantly, they randomized which version was targeted to each student. First, they showed that if the right message could in fact be sent to the right students, impacts on test scores could have been threefold relative to sending everyone the version that worked best on average. In other words, there was huge heterogeneity in which message was predicted to benefit each student the most. Second, they showed that types could be successfully predicted thanks to a previous experiment, which sent only one message to each student still during remote learning – thanks to high-frequency data on how student attendance and online access responded to the intervention back then.

The better screening becomes, the more effective targeting can be. On the flip side, the ability to target very accurately also brings about new ethical dilemmas, especially in connection to data protection. If governments could accurately predict behavioral types, in particular who is likely to conform to social pressure, to be inattentive to price changes or to procrastinate, private companies – from retailers to banks and insurance providers – would love to get hold of this information. If they eventually do, that could lead some types to be exploited by predatory offers or limit their ability to access credit and insurance. There is no obvious way to get around that dilemma: in face of the nature of public sector activity and the likely need to validate such predictions by external committees, it might be hard to reconcile legality with secrecy.

Summary

1. While external conditions might make certain behavioral constraints more important for some (e.g., financial worries capture part of the available bandwidth), biases such as inattention, procrastination, and limiting mental models should, in principle, apply equally to all individuals once differences in their external environment (e.g., their material conditions) are accounted for.
2. That often leads researchers and practitioners to think that interventions to address these biases should target all individuals alike. The truth, however, is that each individual's past trajectory creates unique background and experiences that

produce a rich distribution of behaviors. While this conclusion suggests that successfully confronting persistent public problems by merely augmenting traditional policy tools with behavioral insights might be unlikely, it also sheds light on how true progress could be unlocked: by accurately targeting the right intervention to the right citizen.
3. Naturally, that also brings about new challenges, from the need for scientific evidence on the likely sources of heterogeneity to the ethical dilemmas of having governments screen individual biases and target them with custom interventions.
4. In this chapter, we explored how *heterogeneity* is most likely widespread. Different initial beliefs, combined with different trajectories of exposure to new information, might easily lead to large heterogeneity in how accurate different individuals are at any given point in time – and the more so in the presence of cognitive dissonance. The same logic holds for how inattention and self-control problems might vary dramatically within any target population.
5. Next, we introduced the concept of screening behavioral types. We discussed, under certain conditions, screening is *feasible,* that some biases might be *stable*, and the *best practices* for effective screening strategies.
6. We then discussed whether targeting policies would be feasible within the public sector's institutional constraints, the potential role of technology, its implications for social inequalities, and the new ethical dilemmas it would bring about. Governments already target their citizens, determining who is eligible for certain benefits based on their recent history or even on their traits. Although it is still a gray area of public sector legislation whether one could legally target different policies to different groups based on *invisible features* – since behavioral types cannot ultimately be observed – the truth is, in practice, this already happens in many core dimensions of public life.
7. The better screening becomes, the more effective targeting can be. But effective targeting also brings about new ethical dilemmas. Optimal targeting requires policymakers to trade off the consequences of targeting for addressing externalities with its impacts on social inequalities. Moreover, they must strive to reconcile legality with secrecy so as to prevent individuals from being predated by private companies leveraging public information on citizens' behavioral types.

Suggested Readings

Carvalho, Leandro and Olafsson, Arna and Silverman, Dan, Misfortune and Mistake: The Financial Conditions and Decision-Making Ability of High-Cost Loan Borrowers (September 2019). NBER Working Paper No. w26328, Available at SSRN: https://ssrn.com/abstract=3519734

Olafsson, Arna and Pagel, Michaela, The Ostrich in Us: Selective Attention to Financial Accounts, Income, Spending, and Liquidity (October 2017). NBER Working Paper No. w23945, Available at SSRN: https://ssrn.com/abstract=3057176

Kuchler, Theresa and Pagel, Michaela, Sticking to Your Plan: The Role of Present Bias for Credit Card Paydown (August 2018). NBER Working Paper No. w24881, Available at SSRN: https://ssrn.com/abstract=3226811

Medina, Paolina C. and Pagel, Michaela. Do Savings Nudges Cause Borrowing? Evidence from a Mega Study (2021). NBER WORKING PAPER SERIES No. 28956, available at https://www.nber.org/system/files/working_papers/w28956/w28956.pdf

Stango, Victor and Zinman, Jonathan, Behavioral Biases Are Temporally Stable (September 19, 2020). Available at SSRN: https://ssrn.com/abstract=3695593 or https://doi.org/10.2139/ssrn.3695593

Stango, Victor, and Jonathan Zinman. We are all behavioral, more or less: Measuring and using consumer-level behavioral sufficient statistics. No. w25540. National Bureau of Economic Research, 2019.

Gottlieb, Daniel, and Olivia S. Mitchell. "Narrow framing and long-term care insurance." Journal of Risk and Insurance 87.4 (2020): 861-893.

Lichand, Guilherme, et al. "The impacts of remote learning in secondary education during the pandemic in Brazil." Nature Human Behaviour 6.8 (2022): 1079-1086.

Lichand, Guilherme, and Juliette Thibaud. "Parent-bias." *University of Zurich, Department of Economics, Working Paper* 369 (2020).

Chapter 11
Concluding Remarks: The Future of Policy Design

This book has laid out a new framework for diagnosing behavioral mechanisms behind complex social problems, and for designing policies informed by behavioral insights within the usual tools available to public sector managers. The new framework is mindful of the challenges that brought the original excitement with governmental nudge units to a halt. If it is to promote truly large impacts, it has to go beyond inattention and nudges; and if successful interventions informed by it are to effectively scale, it has to allow policymakers to build on policies that are already in place. The MSI-PRIx framework encompasses both features.

As we emphasized repeatedly throughout the book, accurately diagnosing behavioral problems is at the heart of successful policies that go beyond business-as-usual in addressing externalities and promoting social equality. Such a process is as much science as it is an art form. It requires a combination of different disciplines – psychology, anthropology, sociology, economics, and systems thinking – and, often, multiple rounds of iterative testing.

In our initial applications of this framework, we found that one of the key challenges was not that public managers grappled with new concepts from the MSI framework, or even with their potential applications through the PRIx framework. Rather, the biggest constraint was often that teams were not very open to the idea that they had to explore and iterate, be open to trial and error, and extremely likely to fail (in their diagnostics or in their tentative solutions) at first. That led to insufficient risk-taking, suboptimal exploration, and slow learning. We learned from those experiences that a precondition for using the new framework is setting expectations right from the beginning: sensitizing the relevant teams that their work should be closer to that of a scientist or an experience designer – listening to the target user, testing hypotheses, and trying out different things, rather than quickly trying to jump to solutions.

In writing this book and testing the new framework with real policy teams, we also learned that, even though behavioral sciences and systems thinking do not necessarily come together, embedding behavioral mechanisms in systems and

G. Lichand et al., *Behavioral Insights for Policy Design*,
https://doi.org/10.1007/978-3-031-33034-6_11

subsystems makes it a lot easier to identify promising levers for designing successful interventions. The reason is twofold. First, having to think about the system first forces teams to organize key actors and relations – setting the stage to think next about the behavioral mechanisms that likely mediate these relations. Second, because intervening at any given node might unlock a reinforcement cycle that, in some cases, ultimately renders the original intervention mute or, even worse, sets the system onto a downward spiral. Thinking about the system as a whole forces the team to carefully consider the macro consequences of focused interventions. Perhaps most importantly, it forces the team to constantly monitor the problem – not just the solution –, something that is key in the case of wicked social problems, as its nature is likely to constantly change and adapt to other forces in the system, including the policy intervention itself.

What does the future of behaviorally informed policies look like? As we outlined when discussing heterogeneity, screening, and targeting, there are many open questions linked to best practices in screening behavioral types, the legality of targeting policies to different behavioral profiles, and the use of technology to unlock their largest impacts. Behavioral scientists, legislators, designers, and technology experts will have to collaborate closely to balance the need to improve policy personalization to those linked to protecting vulnerable citizens from the misuse of their data by private sector players, and by government itself.

Summary

1. While the influence of behavioral sciences within both academia and the public sector rapidly expanded in recent years, in order to promote truly transformative impacts, their usage must go beyond inattention and nudges. Moreover, if successful interventions informed by behavioral sciences are to effectively scale, they must allow policymakers to build on policies that are already in place. The MSI-PRIx framework encompasses both features.
2. This book has laid out a new framework for diagnosing behavioral mechanisms behind complex social problems, and for designing policies informed by behavioral insights within the usual tools available to public sector managers. As we emphasized throughout the book, accurately diagnosing behavioral problems is at the heart of successful policies that go the extra mile in addressing externalities and promoting social equality.
3. In the journey that led to this book, we learned several lessons about what likely increases the success of this framework outside of the classroom walls, among which the value of (1) setting expectations right, especially when it comes to the need of adaptive and iterative experimentation; (2) embedding behavioral mechanisms in systems and subsystems, making it a lot easier to identify promising levers for designing successful interventions; and (3) constantly monitoring the problem – not just the solution – as its nature is likely to constantly change and adapt to other forces in the system.

4. Over the previous chapters, we explored what the future of behavioral policy-making might look like. We discussed heterogeneity, screening, and targeting, including best practices in screening types and the legal and technical constraints of targeting policies to different behavioral profiles. This book is only the tip of the iceberg. Scholars and policymakers are only beginning to address many of the key questions involving how design tools and behavioral sciences can be combined in practice to unlock their greatest impacts.
5. If "it takes a village to educate a child," it certainly takes a full mix of professionals to improve policy design. As our discussions have hopefully made it clear, behavioral scientists, designers, legal experts, and ethics specialists must all work together if a government is to effectively address externalities and decrease social inequalities.

Chapter 12
A Toolkit for Policy Teams

Working with public policy is hard work, even more so using new concepts that may seem intimidating at first. That is why tools become an essential item, bringing concepts to practice through visual thinking and collaborative work.

The toolkit presented in this chapter has the purpose to assist the sensemaking process of the public agent who would like to incorporate systems thinking and behavioral insights perspectives into their work. These instruments should not be followed to the letter as a script, but rather as a guide for reflection and, preferably, for group discussions about the challenges at hand and their possible solutions. Examples of how each of these instruments are used in practice were given throughout the book, and will be mentioned here for reference.

12.1 Persona

A persona is a tool developed to profile groups of individuals by characteristics that go beyond sociodemographic ones. What matters here is the behavior that differentiates the groups. In Chap. 6, we presented a differentiation of typical cases and positive deviant individuals. Personas should follow this division, but personas of other agents in the system that are directly involved with the target audience can also be made. Check Table 6.2 in Chap. 6 for an example of persona.

G. Lichand et al., *Behavioral Insights for Policy Design*,
https://doi.org/10.1007/978-3-031-33034-6_12

<table>
<tr><td>Demographics
Name: Maryam
Age: 28</td><td colspan="2">Story
Maryam is a 28-year-old woman married to Ahmad. Maryam and her husband were raised in traditional families where no women worked. But recently, the couple has encountered financial problems and Maryam has started to think about getting a job outside of the home. Ahmad, however, believes that women working outside the home is frowned upon.</td></tr>
<tr><td>Goals
To work outside the home.
To help with the family's bills.
To get approval from her husband.</td><td>Obstacles
Possible stain on husband's reputation.
No close family role models.</td><td>Social Environment
Financial difficulties.
Traditional family.
Few examples of women working outside the home.</td></tr>
</table>

Demographics Relevant sociodemographic characteristics, such as age, name, gender, education, income, and race.

Story A brief story to contextualize the persona. It should reflect the context of the target audience well, although some generalizations are necessary.

Goals Indicate what the goals of the persona are within this context. The goals should be related to the public challenge.

Obstacles What is preventing the persona from realizing these goals? They can be intrinsic or extrinsic.

Social Environment What other issues in the environment are relevant to the persona's goals or obstacles?

Demographics	**Story**	
Goals	**Obstacles**	**Social Environment**

12.2 Storyboard

A storyboard represents the trajectory of a persona in a system. This tool is intended to highlight the challenges that a typical case agent faces when living with a public problem. Similarly, it also shows the strategies of positive deviants when solving the problem in some capacity, generating insights about behavioral mechanisms and possible solutions. Check Table 6.3 in Chap. 6 for an example of a storyboard.

Scene 1	Scene 2	Scene 3
Maryam and her husband Ahmad are having financial problems.	To help, Maryam started thinking about working outside the home and saw some job offers for women.	But Maryam has never worked and doesn't know any women that work.
Scene 4	**Scene 5**	**Scene 6**
Still, Maryam decided to propose the idea to her husband, hoping to get his approval.	When she proposed the idea, Ahmad responded that most husbands do not approve of their wives working and that it might be frowned upon by other men.	Ahmad, although not personally against it, rejects Maryam's idea because he believes that his relatives and peers would not approve of Maryam working outside the home.

Writing Storyboards In each scene, write the story of the persona going through the system and experiencing the public problem at hand. Try to highlight important moments and give details that help understand their challenge. Each storyboard has six scenes, but they can have more or less, depending on the complexity of the story that must be told. Remember to make a storyboard for each relevant persona in the system.

Scene 1	Scene 2	Scene 3
Scene 4	**Scene 5**	**Scene 6**

12.3 Naming Variables

Identifying and naming variables is a sensemaking exercise and therefore takes time and thought. To facilitate this process, the persona and storyboard tools can help by providing snippets that can be transformed into relevant variables. In a first step, it is recommended to identify all possible variables, even if not all of them will be used. This process helps in modeling the system, since the variety of variables available helps in thinking about the system. Check Table 6.5 in Chap. 6 for an example of variable naming.

"Ahmad, although not personally against it, rejects Maryam's idea because he believes that his relatives and peers do not approve of Maryam working outside the home."	
Excerpt	**Variable**
"not personally against it"	personal approval of husbands
"rejects"	de facto approval of husbands
"believes that his relatives and peers do not approve"	perceived social disapproval
"Maryam working outside the home"	women in the labor force

Choose a snippet and place it at the top. Then, identify excerpts and try to turn them into variables from the following rules:

Name Variables as Quantities That Can Vary The dynamic aspect of CLD means especially the changes in variables, as they rise or fall, grow or decline.

Use Nouns Verbs and actions are conveyed in the arrows, so they should be avoided.

Separate Perceptions from Actual States Sometimes it is useful to include perceptions on the CLD, but they should be signaled to clarify the role of each variable in the diagrams.

Snippet	
Excerpt	**Variable**

12.4 Building a Map

Drawing a systemic map is an iterative process, made up of multiple successions of modeling, reflection, and adjustments. It is recommended to start with a large map, with many variables and connections. From this map, you can prioritize what is essential to explain the challenge. Think of a complete story and then a summary: what are the essential items that explain the story? Apply this logic to map building to generate good systemic models. Check Figs. 6.1 through 6.5 in Chap. 6 for an example of map building.

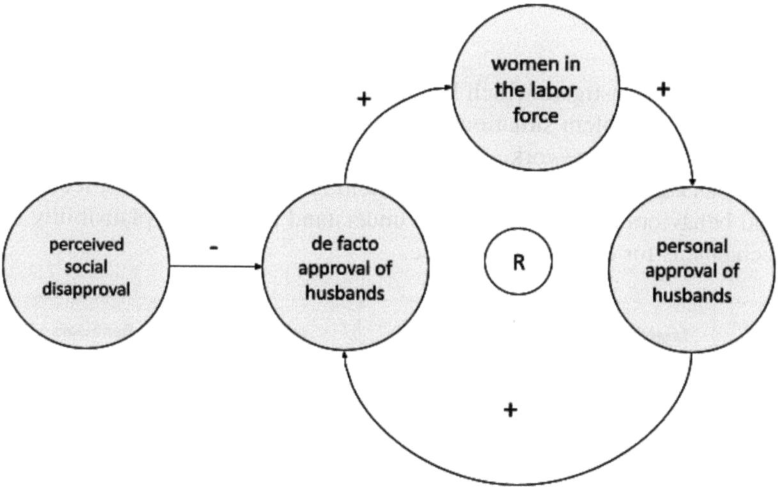

A map emerges from the variables identified in the Naming Variables tool. It is important to check that the map constructed is consistent with the storyboard and the personas.

Be careful when building a very complex map. It must be explainable, that is, the relationships between variables must be clear and feedback loops, evident. Maps that are too complex do not help to identify possible leverage points for the solution of a problem.

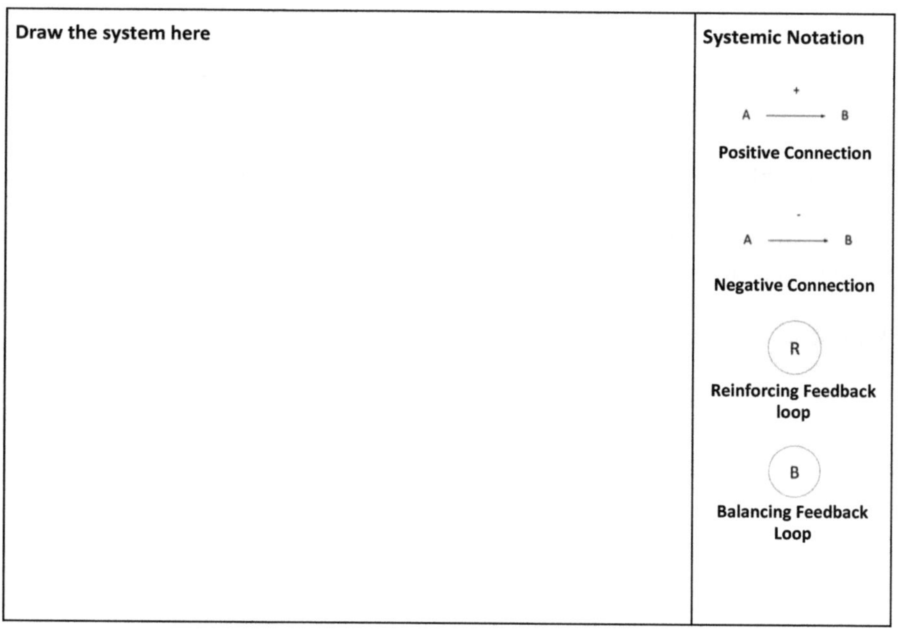

12.5 Vignettes

Vignettes are tools to investigate which behavioral mechanisms of the MSI framework are prevalent in problem situations and even to experiment with some solutions from the PRIx framework. Vignettes are short stories that illustrate problem situations across different scenarios, eliciting characters' beliefs, feelings, intentions and behaviors in each scenario to understand the relative plausibility of different mechanisms for our target audience.

Public Problem	Target audience	Mechanisms	Attitudes	Behaviors
Economically active women in Saudi Arabia cannot work outside the home without challenging social norms and obtaining the approval of their male "guardians."	**Audience** Male "guardians"of economically active Saudi women	Social expectations	Women working is culturally frowned upon	Prevents his wife from working
	Environment Household	Social image concerns	Worrying about what other husbands will think He is in favor of my wife working	More likely to allow his wife to work

Public Problem Statement that determines the public problem at hand.

Target Audience (i) Audience who will answer the questions in the vignette; (ii) Environment in which the vignette situations take place.

Attitudes The emotions and intentions related to the situations in the vignette.

Behavior The behaviors actually adopted.

Public Problem	Target audience	Mechanisms	Attitudes	Behaviors
	Audience			
	Environment			

12.6 MSI-PRIx Board

The board is designed to assist in the processes of investigating the behavioral mechanisms (from the MSI framework) and of formulating tentative solutions informed by these insights (from the PRIx framework) for the problem at hand. Essentially, the board is an investigative "game" in which the hypothesis behind the social problem must be analyzed according to the questions at each stage of the board.

Motivation problems

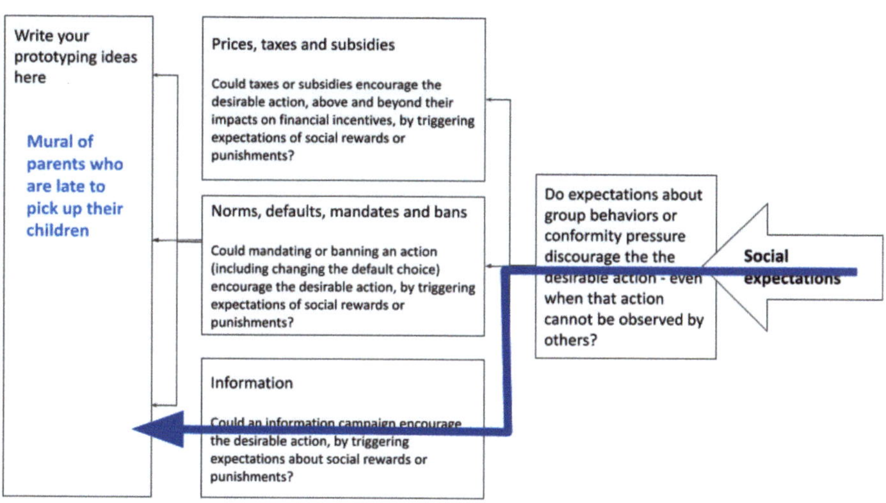

Choose a Hypothesis Select a hypothesis to work on. From it, start the "game" on one of the mechanisms you think is most likely.

Work Through the Questions From the questions in each square, ask whether the hypothesis matches it. If yes, move forward one step.

Brainstorm Solution Ideas Starting from the PRIx framework, propose solutions for the most promising mechanisms. Then analyze and prioritize the most feasible ones.

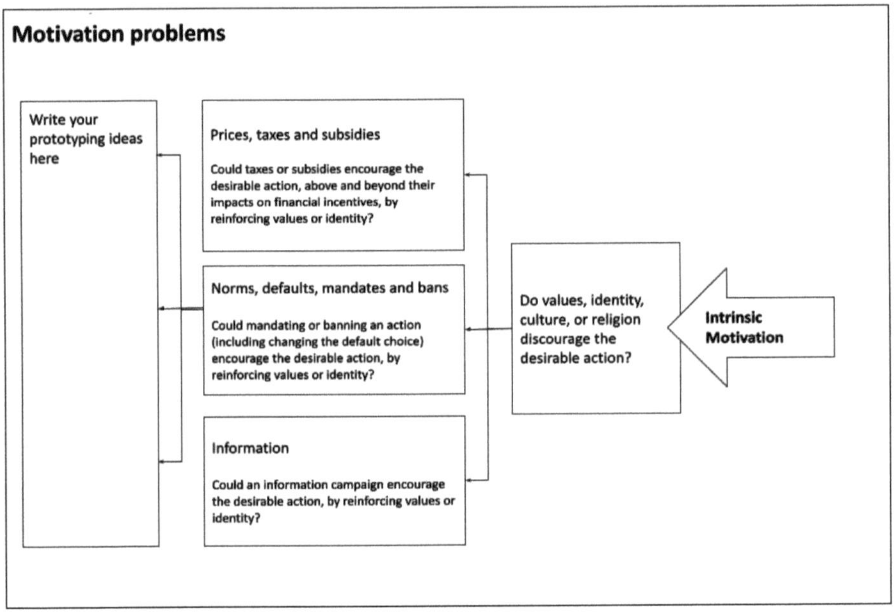

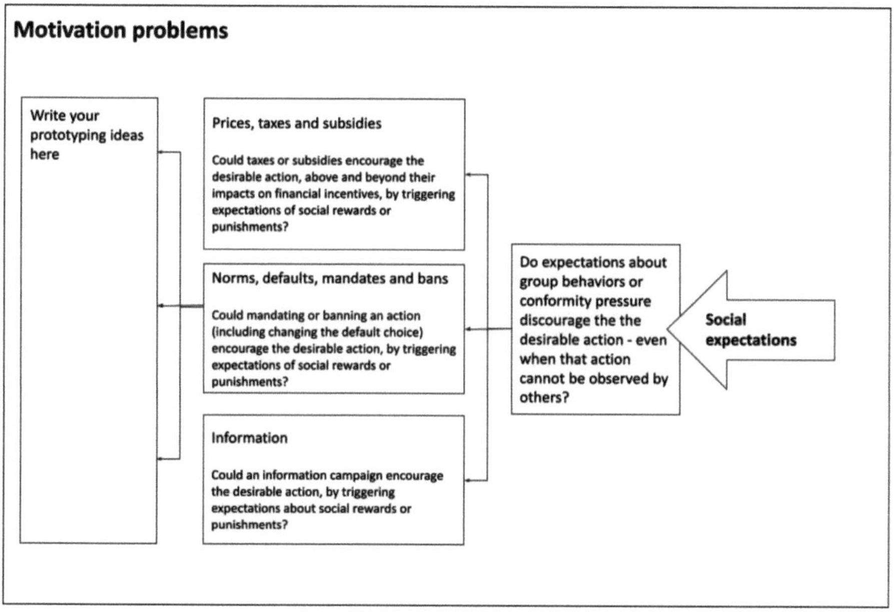
Motivation problems
Write your prototyping ideas here
Prices, taxes and subsidies
Could taxes or subsidies encourage the desirable action, above and beyond their impacts on financial incentives, by triggering expectations of social rewards or punishments?
Norms, defaults, mandates and bans
Could mandating or banning an action (including changing the default choice) encourage the desirable action, by triggering expectations of social rewards or punishments?
Information
Could an information campaign encourage the desirable action, by triggering expectations about social rewards or punishments?
Do expectations about group behaviors or conformity pressure discourage the the desirable action - even when that action cannot be observed by others?
Social expectations

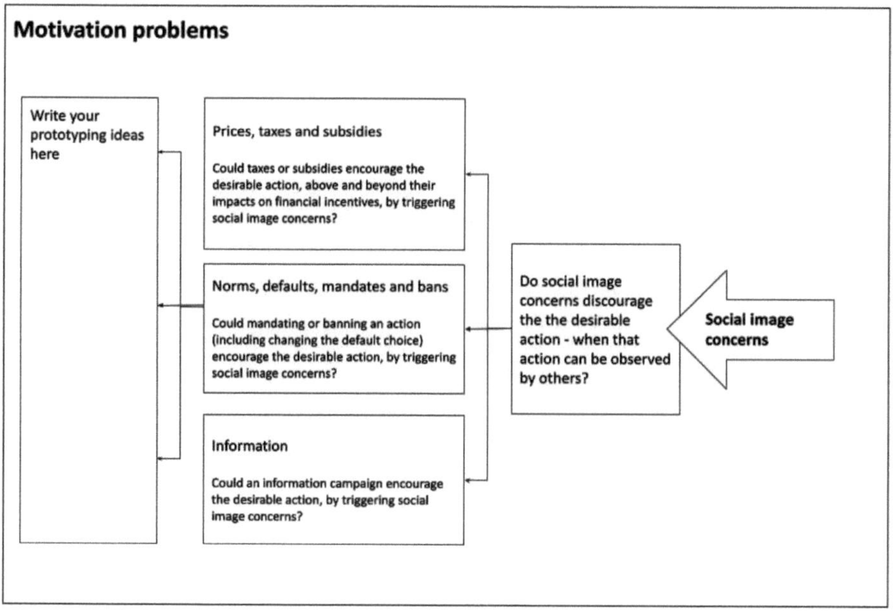
Motivation problems
Write your prototyping ideas here
Prices, taxes and subsidies
Could taxes or subsidies encourage the desirable action, above and beyond their impacts on financial incentives, by triggering social image concerns?
Norms, defaults, mandates and bans
Could mandating or banning an action (including changing the default choice) encourage the desirable action, by triggering social image concerns?
Information
Could an information campaign encourage the desirable action, by triggering social image concerns?
Do social image concerns discourage the the desirable action - when that action can be observed by others?
Social image concerns

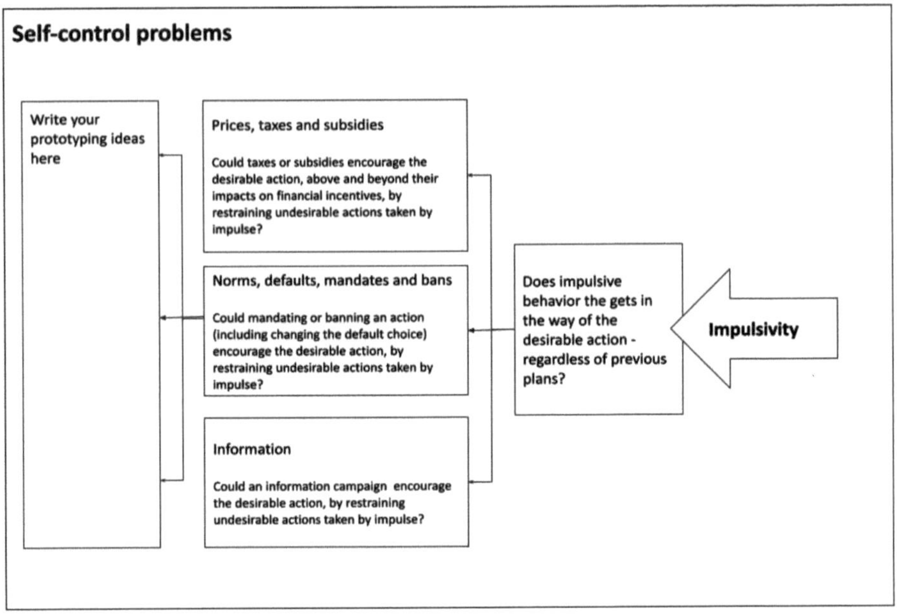
Self-control problems
Write your prototyping ideas here
Prices, taxes and subsidies
Could taxes or subsidies encourage the desirable action, above and beyond their impacts on financial incentives, by restraining undesirable actions taken by impulse?
Norms, defaults, mandates and bans
Could mandating or banning an action (including changing the default choice) encourage the desirable action, by restraining undesirable actions taken by impulse?
Information
Could an information campaign encourage the desirable action, by restraining undesirable actions taken by impulse?
Does impulsive behavior the gets in the way of the desirable action - regardless of previous plans?
Impulsivity

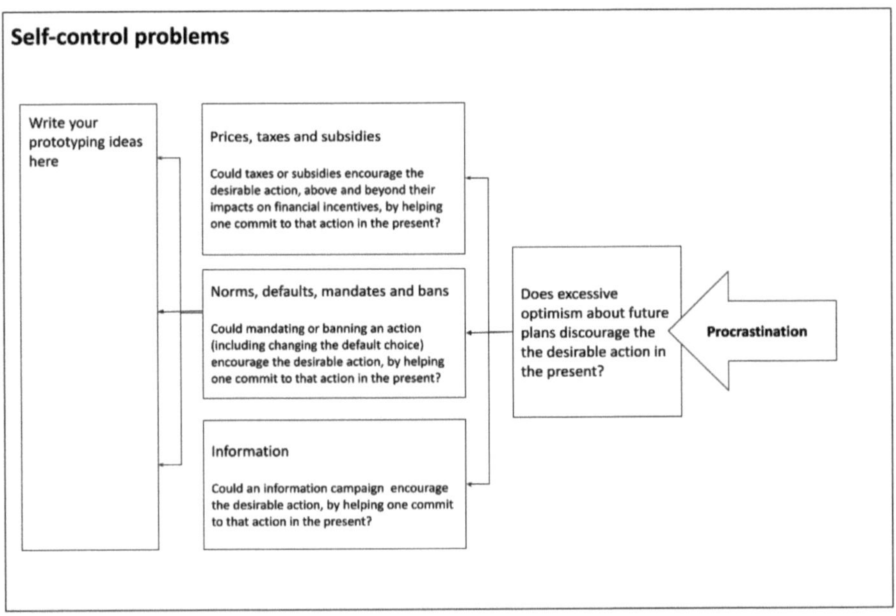
Self-control problems
Write your prototyping ideas here
Prices, taxes and subsidies
Could taxes or subsidies encourage the desirable action, above and beyond their impacts on financial incentives, by helping one commit to that action in the present?
Norms, defaults, mandates and bans
Could mandating or banning an action (including changing the default choice) encourage the desirable action, by helping one commit to that action in the present?
Information
Could an information campaign encourage the desirable action, by helping one commit to that action in the present?
Does excessive optimism about future plans discourage the the desirable action in the present?
Procrastination

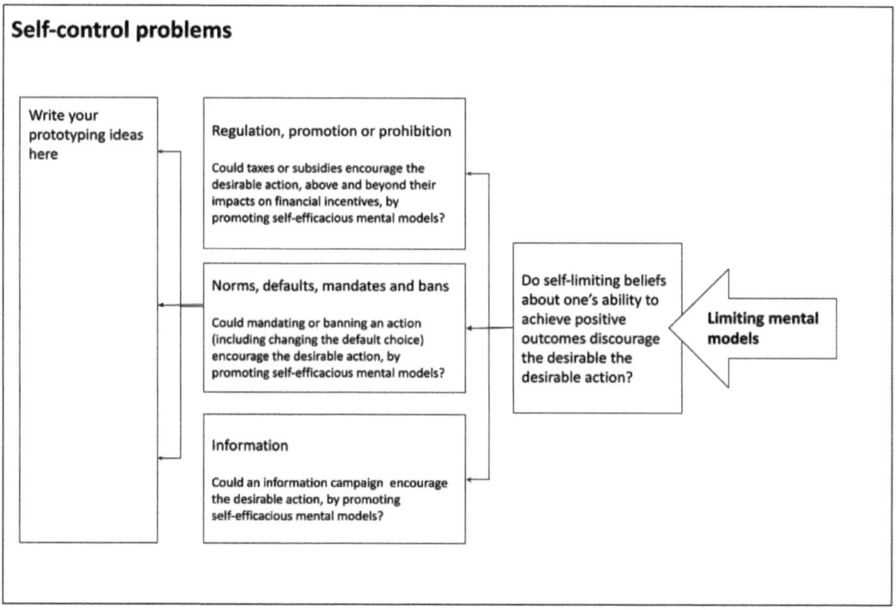
Self-control problems
Write your prototyping ideas here
Regulation, promotion or prohibition
Could taxes or subsidies encourage the desirable action, above and beyond their impacts on financial incentives, by promoting self-efficacious mental models?
Norms, defaults, mandates and bans
Could mandating or banning an action (including changing the default choice) encourage the desirable action, by promoting self-efficacious mental models?
Information
Could an information campaign encourage the desirable action, by promoting self-efficacious mental models?
Do self-limiting beliefs about one's ability to achieve positive outcomes discourage the desirable the desirable action?
Limiting mental models

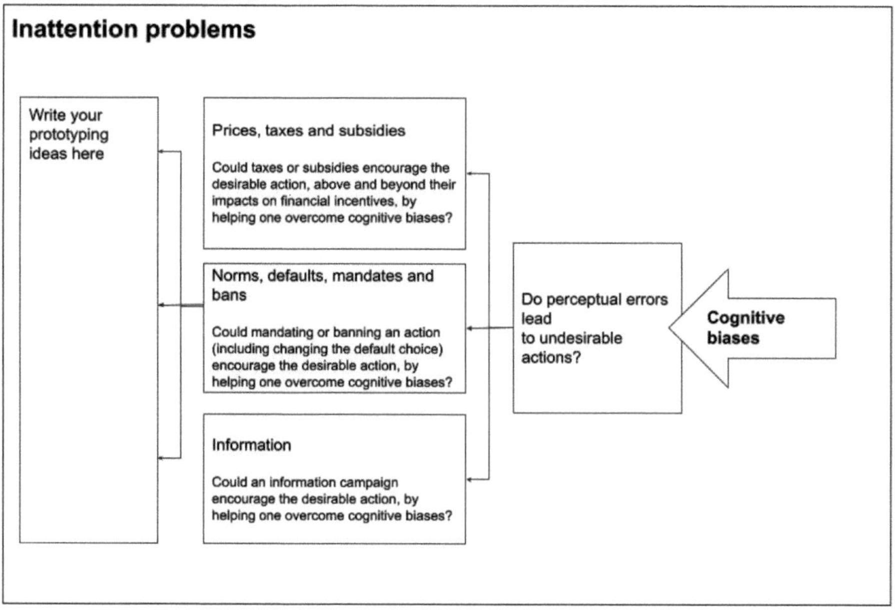
Inattention problems
Write your prototyping ideas here
Prices, taxes and subsidies
Could taxes or subsidies encourage the desirable action, above and beyond their impacts on financial incentives, by helping one overcome cognitive biases?
Norms, defaults, mandates and bans
Could mandating or banning an action (including changing the default choice) encourage the desirable action, by helping one overcome cognitive biases?
Information
Could an information campaign encourage the desirable action, by helping one overcome cognitive biases?
Do perceptual errors lead to undesirable actions?
Cognitive biases

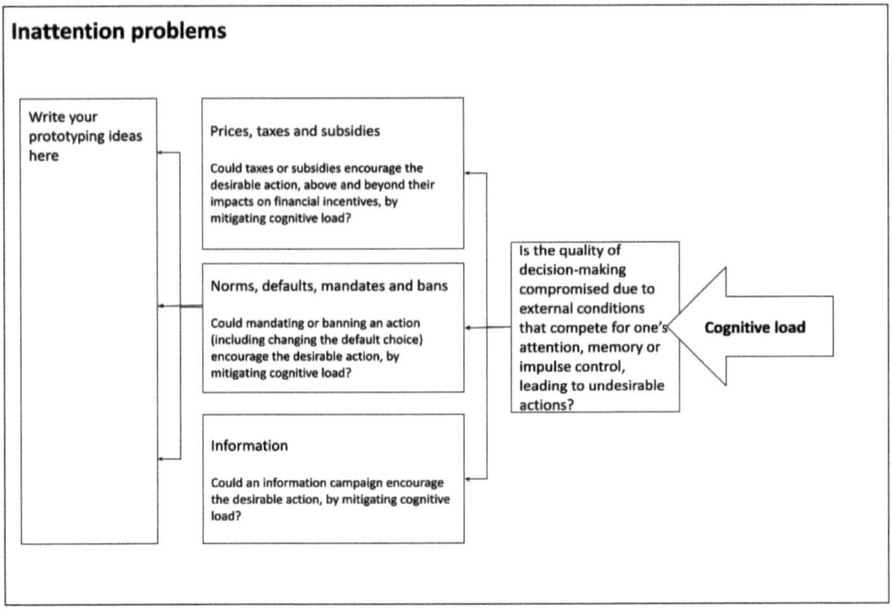
Inattention problems
Write your prototyping ideas here
Prices, taxes and subsidies
Could taxes or subsidies encourage the desirable action, above and beyond their impacts on financial incentives, by mitigating cognitive load?
Norms, defaults, mandates and bans
Could mandating or banning an action (including changing the default choice) encourage the desirable action, by mitigating cognitive load?
Information
Could an information campaign encourage the desirable action, by mitigating cognitive load?
Is the quality of decision-making compromised due to external conditions that compete for one's attention, memory or impulse control, leading to undesirable actions?
Cognitive load

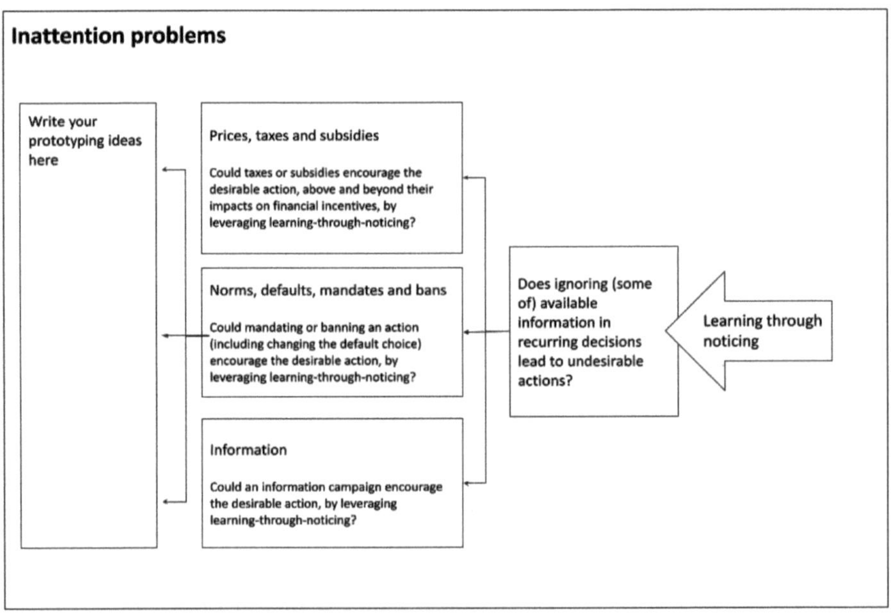
Inattention problems
Write your prototyping ideas here
Prices, taxes and subsidies
Could taxes or subsidies encourage the desirable action, above and beyond their impacts on financial incentives, by leveraging learning-through-noticing?
Norms, defaults, mandates and bans
Could mandating or banning an action (including changing the default choice) encourage the desirable action, by leveraging learning-through-noticing?
Information
Could an information campaign encourage the desirable action, by leveraging learning-through-noticing?
Does ignoring (some of) available information in recurring decisions lead to undesirable actions?
Learning through noticing

Summary

1. This chapter provides supporting materials for identifying variables in systems and subsystems, for diagnosing plausible behavioral mechanisms behind social problems, for testing which behavioral mechanisms are more likely for the problem at hand, and for augmenting policies with these behavioral insights.
2. These toolkit is meant as a simple starting point for policy teams working on real social problems. All processes are meant to be iterative, whereby the team reevaluates previous hypotheses in face of new evidence, updating the plausibility and feasibility of competing mechanisms and refining policy prototypes informed by these tentative insights.
3. The interested reader should refer to the suggested readings of each chapter for additional resources.

Index

G. Lichand et al., *Behavioral Insights for Policy Design*,
https://doi.org/10.1007/978-3-031-33034-6

MIX
Papier aus verantwortungsvollen Quellen
Paper from responsible sources
FSC® C105338

If you have any concerns about our products,
you can contact us on
ProductSafety@springernature.com

In case Publisher is established outside the EU,
the EU authorized representative is:
Springer Nature Customer Service Center GmbH
Europaplatz 3, 69115 Heidelberg, Germany

Printed by Libri Plureos GmbH
in Hamburg, Germany